WORKPLACE DEMOCRATIZATION

WORKPLACE DEMOCRATIZATION

Its Internal Dynamics

Paul Bernstein

Transaction Books
New Brunswick, New Jersey

Library of Congress Catalog Number: 79-66569
ISBN: 0-87855-711-3 (paper)
Printed in the United States of America

Library of Congress Cataloging in Publication Data

Bernstein, Paul, 1945-
　Workplace democratization, its internal dynamics.

　Reprint of the 1976 ed. published by the Comparative Administration Research Institute, Kent, Ohio.
　Bibliography: p.
　Includes index.
　1. Employees' representation in management.
2. Plywood industry—United States—Employees.
I. Title.
[HD5650.B38 1979]　　658.31'52'0973　　79-66569
ISBN 0-87855-711-3

To the memory of
J. Palach of Czechoslovakia,
S.A. of Chile,
and others unknown,
whose lives were ended prematurely
in the pursuit of democratization.

ACKNOWLEDGEMENTS

I am deeply grateful to a large number of people who aided me during the several stages this work passed through: Marjorie Young, whose friendship was strong sustenance during the period of initial investigation of case studies; the worker-owners in Oregon and Washington who allowed me to inspect their plywood mills and willingly answered my many questions; Stanford University Professors Robert C. North, Charles Drekmeier, W. Richard Scott, Yosal Rogat, John Gurley, and John Barton, who set high standards and offered many helpful clarifications when this research had developed into a doctoral dissertation form; Professor Douglas Parker of California State University at Long Beach, who lent his precise, professional guidance at crucial points; Betsy Bridgman, graduate student, colleague, and friend at the University of California (Irvine), for her detailed criticism and evaluation of several drafts; Bill Behn and his colleagues at the Center for Economic Studies (Palo Alto, California), who shared with me many important source materials.

My appreciation is deep for several friends whose encouragement, advice, good sense, and warmth aided the endeavor and whose typing and proofreading labors on the manuscript were indispensable: Karen Lundegaard, Peggy Tramel Popovich, Viviane Wayne, Gayle Hill, Mary Rezich, Martha Hauk, Jeff Tasher, and David Ashen.

For comments that improved the style of the text and saved me from committing several errors in print I am grateful to Nancy Lyons, co-editor of *Working Papers for a New Society* (Cambridge, Mass.); Professors James Hunt, College of Business Administration, Southern Illinois University; George W. England, Industrial Relations Center, University of Minnesota; Ichak Adizes, Graduate School of Management, UCLA; and three colleagues at my present institution, David Stodolsky, Robert Dubin, and Willi Schonfeld. Of course, I am entirely responsible for any errors that managed to pass through that sieve.

A somewhat longer version of Chapter 2 was published in *Working Papers for a New Society*, 2:24–34. The permission to reprint sections of that article granted by the editors and publisher is gratefully acknowledged.

Financial support for certain portions of the research was kindly granted by the International Studies Committee of Stanford University (Bob Jones, Director) and the Graduate Council of the University of California, Irvine (Arnold Binder, Chairman).

Finally, I am deeply grateful to Dr. Anant R. Negandhi, Director of the Comparative Administration Research Institute at Kent State University, for his special help and support in guiding this work to press.

CONTENTS

LIST OF FIGURES

Page

LIST OF TABLES

Towards a Model of
Workplace Democratization

Modern industrialized societies are experiencing a growing interest in ways to make worklife more meaningful and satisfying to the worker. Experiments are being undertaken, conferences are being held, unions and corporations are being confronted by new demands from young workers, and the media are beginning to convey this activity to the public via cover-stories and special T.V. documentaries (HEW, 1973; Davis, Cherns, et al., 1975; *Newsweek*, 1973).

Actually, this is not a new concern. Ever since the advent of the factory system over a century ago, people have been attempting experimental forms for managing production in ways alternative to the strictly hierarchical, sometimes even autocratic, conventional forms. Nineteenth-century communes (Holloway, 1966; Nordhoff, 1972), socialist and anarchist movements (Lichtheim, 1969), and several employer-initiated reforms (Lauck, 1926) sought more egalitarian and democratic means to manage society's unavoidable basic task of production.

Only recently, however, has this vast experience begun to be analyzed together. For a long time, the particular ideology of each movement inclined it to distrust the specific forms and goals of others. Marxist writers, for instance, seldom gave attention to partial cases of democratization. They objected to the presence of the original private owner, even though his power was reduced. Working by a similar logic, some early workplace reformers in America hesitated to synthesize their own experience with that of socialist experiments in other countries such as the Soviet Union, assuming all of those to be, *ipso facto*, false fronts for autocratic party control.

Within the academic world traditional disciplinary boundaries of specialization between, for example, political historians and industrial psychologists tended to keep the total experience dispersed. In the business world many individual cases remained isolated because each was regarded by those who had contact with it as a unique occurrence, so unusual, that it was not considered seriously as suggesting an alternative model in general for industrial management. For example, the Bat'a system of worker self-administration and productivity sharing (described in Chapter 3) went generally unknown for over forty years, although the company itself became a worldwide conglomerate and was one of the few to expand production and sales during both the depression of the 1920s in Europe and the worldwide Depression of the 1930s. Likewise, the nearly two dozen worker-owned plywood mills in America's Pacific Northwest that have been in successful operation for nearly twenty years were studied at length by only two scholars (Berman, 1967; Bellas, 1972) and had not been analyzed in the context of a comparative study of workplace democratization.

Now, in the last few years, useful comparative studies have begun to appear. Each uses a different data base, with some overlaps of course, and each has approached those data with different ends in view. For example, Carole Pateman in *Participation and Democratic Theory* (1970) criticizes prevailing theories of stable national democracy (notably those of Schumpeter and H. Eckstein) which rely on *lack* of participation by the masses for their stability. She argues that evidence from workplace democracy in several European companies supports a more participatory theory for stable democracy. In another recent study, *Industrial Democracy: The Sociology of Participation*, Paul Blumberg (1968) assembles the many social-psychology experiments that have involved partial participation by workers in management. He argues that their general results—increased worker satisfaction with their jobs and often increased productivity for their firms— imply a workable solution to the persistent problem of job alienation.

At this early stage of comparative study, it can be expected that not all possible advantages of multiple-case analysis have yet been utilized. In particular, it could be used advantageously to derive a general inductive model. The need for such a model has been emphasized by Mulder (1973: 219) and Dunn (1973:195–220). Furthermore, Dunlop has stated that generally the study of labor-management relations suffers from "a mountain of facts and a glut of raw material," needing an "integrating theory, which has lagged far behind the expansion of experience" (1973:115). One helpful way to begin the process of integrating empirical experience is by inductive model building.

The aim of this study is to begin construction of a model of workplace democratization. By "model" we understand a set of specified units, a description of their interactions, and a delimitation of their boundaries as a system. Together such an assemblage is intended to represent symbolically a specified portion of reality (Miller, 1965: 202–209; Dubin, 1975). The model-building process in the present research is inductive: we assemble a broad range of empirical cases, analyze them for their underlying principles, and generate a minimal set of fundamental components. We then elucidate the nature of each of these components and examine the major interactions between them. Moreover, we utilize the information gained from this first-stage model to explain some major reasons for the success or failure of democratization in specific instances.

DEFINING GENERAL TERMS

Since this field is still a relatively new one, a standardized lexicon does not yet exist. Rather, one encounters many, and sometimes contradictory, uses of even the most basic terms. It is necessary, therefore, to establish at the outset the meaning of several basic terms.

The title "workplace democratization" has been chosen and "democratization" is used as the central concept throughout. Alternative terms for the same general area in common use elsewhere are industrial democracy, self-management, workers' control, or participation, but each has connotations, ambiguities, or other difficulties rendering them inappropriate to our focus.

Workers' control usually implies full worker hegemony over the firm or even the entire economy. Coates and Topham of the British Institute for Workers' Control argue for confining the term to this meaning (Coates and Topham, 1968). However, workers' control has also been used to mean only the gradual acquisition of such power, a strategy which includes many stages of partial power along the way, as in the writings of the French theorist Andre Gorz (1967) or the Spanish experience in Catalonia (Souchy, 1965:82; Dolgoff, 1974). In the interest of clarity we have avoided frequent use of this term in the present study and have endeavored when using it to indicate which meaning is intended—the final state or the process of development. It is not used as the central concept and title here because it implies a permanent subordination of the rights of managers. It seemed advisable to begin a scientific inquiry with a more neutral perspective.

A second term used to cover the entire field, "participation," tends toward vagueness and is subject to a host of interpretations. Among European writers a certain consensus has been forming which assigns participation to the lesser forms of worker influence in management (Coates and Topham, 1968; Karlsson, 1973). These authors argue that where managers retain final control the employee is merely *participating* in a consultative process; he is not really self-governing. Above that level, they argue that other terms must be applied, such as workers' control. Yet the consensus is not a solid one, for influential writers like sociologist Paul Blumberg and political theorist Carole Pateman use participation to cover the entire range of worker influence in decision-making. And in between, there are writers like French, Israel, and Aas (1960:3) who prefer to confine the term participation to those situations that involve only joint decision-making. They would, therefore, exclude both the experience of final managerial control with prior consultation of workers and the experience of total worker control which Blumberg and Pateman include.

Two other basic terms, "self-management" and "industrial democracy," would seem to be more attractive candidates. The first is favored by writers influenced by the Yugoslav experience (Kmetic, 1967; Denitch, 1972; Vanek, 1975), but it has been criticized for connoting mere psychological self-control (management of the self) especially to those unfamiliar with the area. To solve that problem it has sometimes been expanded to "workers' self-management." However, the objection can then be raised that it either ignores managers or subordinates them to permanent second-class status. Industrial democracy avoids both those difficulties, but as we wish to develop the model beyond industry to other workplaces—the office, the school, etc.—we have settled on the more inclusive term "workplace democratization." Also workplace is more appropriate than industrial for this study because our focus remains within the organization, while industrial democracy often includes relations between organizations.

The object of this study, workplace democratization, includes any system which attempts to increase employee influence in the management process, especially in decision-making. This influence can range from a manager's solicitation of employee opinions to complete worker autonomy in running a wholly worker-owned firm.

Finally, the question of why choose the word "democratization" instead of simply democracy? The major reason is that the present study is concerned with the *process of transformation* a workplace undergoes as it moves toward more democracy, not just the particular democracy it may eventually achieve. Secondly, the emphasis on process that is inevitable with the term democratization seems more realistic for the long run. It helps to keep us aware of the fact that, in all probability, there is no fixed, single, or final state of workplace democracy. The illusion that there is such a fixed form has often led to rigid, unworkable systems (Lauck, 1926). Lastly, the term democratization has begun to be utilized by other researchers in the field (Gustavsen, 1973: 5–22), and it best emphasizes the focus on politics within the organization, the sharing of power phenomenon, which is the central perspective in our analysis. (In the body of the text, democratization is used as a generic term and the other aforementioned possibilities, such as self-management, workers' control, and participation, in more specific meanings. The inductive process followed gives more grounding for each term than would continuation of an *a priori* discussion.)

CRITERIA FOR DATA COLLECTION

This study begins with the description and analysis of several empirical cases. They range from very minor departures from the prevailing management system to wholly worker-owned and worker-managed firms. This wide range was preferred because of our aim to derive a general model, not deductively from a particular theory or two, but inductively from as diverse a set of concrete experiences as could be examined within a reasonable period. It seemed important to try to overcome the problems of isolation and ideological barriers that had long plagued the field. To this end, we tried not to start with too rigid a preconceived theoretical position, and instead allowed new case material to force revisions and redirections of the model. We tried to give serious attention to almost any case claiming to provide workplace democratization and then analyzed it for the elements it might contribute to building and complicating the model.

Even with this broad intent, certain decision-rules had to be established in selecting case material. We made our selection according to these three rules:

1. Autonomous firms received priority over state authorized and initiated systems;
2. Our examination was restricted to companies organized for profit, leaving out subsidized places of employment such as hospitals or government bureaucracies;
3. Pure enterprises received priority over the communitarian mixtures of enterprise-and-residential community.

Let us explain our reasoning behind each of these decisions. State initiated and authorized systems of workplace democratization, such as those which occur in Yugoslavia (Hunnius, 1973:268–321) or China (Bettelheim, 1974) or which did occur at one time in Algeria (I. Clegg, 1971), present special problems of authority and management. Workers there not only have to share power with professional managers but also have to respond to frequent pressures from state or party authorities. Further, the state may claim that its intervention into the governance of these firms is to protect or to represent the interests of yet a third constituency: the general public or "society as a whole" (including the future generation). These factors require special study, and it seemed prudent to begin the task of model-construction with the simpler phenomenon of the autonomous enterprise.

Our second restriction was taken also in the interest of simplifying the number of factors involved in this stage of model construction. Subsidized places of employment often are engaged in service occupations (e.g., medicine or social work) which may give the organization and its members significantly different goals and self-conceptions compared to companies engaged in production for profit. Secondly, the dependence of subsidized organizations on an outside institution for their extra resources (whether that be private or governmental) adds a complicating factor to the internal relations of authority and decision-making.

A third class of democratized enterprises given minimal attention here was the communitarian enterprise, e.g., the Israeli kibbutz (Fine, 1973) or the Oneida industrial community in New York (Holloway, 1966: 179–197). These firms are enmeshed in wider relations, but not just at the top of their structures as are the subsidized organizations and the state-systems. In the communitarian systems, every member has the interests not only of an employee, but also of a neighbor and resident. These additional roles bring specific loyalties and expectations. Usually these communities also have very strong ideologies that significantly govern the members' behavior, and subordinate the enterprise as a whole to goals and values defined by the community at large. For these reasons, it seemed wise to recognize these cases as a somewhat different phenomenon from pure enterprises in a heterogeneous society. (Interesting work comparing communitarian with autonomous democratized firms can be found in Adizes [1971], who reports not only on the Israeli experience but also the "industrial communities" recently established by the new Peruvian regime.) Nevertheless, where these very differences of communitarian firms allowed us to glimpse possible new directions of development for intra-firm dynamics in democratization, we sought ways to allow those insights to inform the general model. That same approach was used in handling data available from some of the state-authorized systems of democratization. In those cases the pressure of an external authority has sometimes forced the development of the firm's internal relations between worker and manager onto new paths which were found useful for possible enrichment of the model. Specifically, we considered those perspectives when they seemed able a) to increase the model's capacity to anticipate possible future developments, or b) to illustrate alternative democratic modes of internal functioning. Table 1.1 summarizes the cases of democratization used for the data base.

Table 1.1

CASES OF DEMOCRATIZATION EXAMINED

Type	Case and Country	Sources
I. Autonomous Firms	Worker-owned plywood companies—USA	1. Personal on-site investigation [Bernstein, 1974] 2. Berman 3. Bellas
	Scott-Bader Commonwealth—UK	1. Blum 2. Farrow, 1968b
	American Cast Iron Pipe Co.—USA	1. Bentley 2. Employees' Manual 3. Zwerdling
	John Lewis Partnership—UK	1. Farrow, 1968a 2. Flanders et al.
	Bat'a Boot & Shoe Co.—Czechoslovakia	1. Dubreuil 2. International Labor Office 3. Sprague 4. Čekota 5. Hindus
	Scanlon Plan companies—USA	1. Lesieur (ed.) 2. Frost et al.
	Works Councils—USA (1919–1930)	1. Derber 2. National Industrial Conference Board 3. Douglas
	Polish Works Councils[2]	Kolaja, 1960
	Democratization experiments—Norway	1. Blumberg 2. Jenkins 3. Gustavsen
	Participation, work redesign and job enrichment experiments—USA	1. U.S. Dept. of HEW 2. Blumberg 3. Gouldner 4. Jenkins
	British job redesign (Tavistock experiments)	Emery and Trist
	Histadrut Union Enterprises—Israel	1. Fine 2. Tabb and Goldfarb
	Imperial Chemical Industries—UK	*Business Week Magazine*, 1971
II. Communitarian	Spanish anarchist collectives (1936–39)	Dolgoff (ed.)

Table 1.1 (*Cont.*)

Type	Case and Country	Sources
II. Com- muni- tarian (cont.)	Israeli kibbutzim and moshavim	1. Personal interviews 2. Fine 3. Goldfarb and Tabb
	19th Century American communes	1. Nordhoff 2. Holloway
III. State- Author- ized Systems	Czechoslovak mines (1920–1939)	1. Papanek 2. Bloss
	Most Czechoslovak industry (1945–1948)	Hindus
	(1968–1969)	1. Personal interviews 2. Remington (ed.) 3. Stradal
	British Nationalized industries	1. H. Clegg 2. Barratt-Brown
	Codetermination in coal and steel industries—West Germany	1. Blumenthal 2. McKitterick and Roberts 3. Sturmthal 1964 4. Schuchman
	French Works Councils and worker-directors	Sturmthal 1964
	Works Councils—Belgium	Potvin
	Works Councils—Germany	Sturmthal, 1964
	Works Councils—Norway	1. *agenor* (magazine) 2. Blumberg
	Yugoslav self-management	1. Sturmthal 1964 2. Hunnius 3. Blumberg 4. Rus 5. Kolaja, 1965 6. Flaes 7. Gorupić and Paj 8. Obradović 9. Adizes, 1973
	Swedish industrial democracy	1. H. Bernstein 2. Karlsson 3. Therborn (per. comm.) 4. Norcross
	U.S. labor unions[1]	1. Derber 2. Sturmthal 1970 3. Personal interviews

Table 1.1 (*Cont.*)

Type	Case and Country	Sources
III. State-Author-ized Systems (cont.)	Canadian Provincial enterprises	1. Shearer 2. *Business Week Magazine*, 1975 3. NDP News 4. Wilson
	Soviet Industry	1. Brinton 2. Mallet 3. Personal interviews
	Chinese enterprises	1. Richman 2. Myrdal 3. Macciocchi 4. Bettelheim
	Algerian workers' councils	I. Clegg

Notes: 1. This case is state-*enabled* but is not required by law.
2. These were autonomously initiated by the firms' employees, although later restricted by the state (Type III).

CONSTRUCTION OF THE MODEL

The aim in constructing a model was to keep it as simple as possible, yet we also wanted it to apply to as broad a range of cases as possible. Dunn emphasizes the difficulties involved in this, given the diversity and immense number of cases. He concludes that "the problems of generalizing formal characteristics of self-management are formidable" (Dunn, 1973: 199).

Our strategy for dealing with this problem was to be very stringent in selecting components to fill the model. They were examined one at a time, and each was allowed to enter the model only if the case material showed it to be necessary for the maintenance of democratization. To implement this strategy we had to make clear what would constitute "the maintenance of democratization." Since our method was to be inductive and we were to be deriving the content of the definition, we could not assert it *a priori*. Rather, all we could do was to establish explicit criteria of performance that such a full definition would have to meet, and then seek elements in the data that could meet those criteria. This would become our elaborate definition in the future, and would at the same time specify a first-stage model.

The criteria we settled on are as follows:

1. The first necessity is that the organization be viable, that functionally and economically it can sustain itself through time. This means it must be profit-making over the average of a reasonable length of time (five-year spans are suitable). And it means that the system of governance, too, must have its own viability; it must have a self-reinforcing, self-sustaining (cybernetic) character.

2. Our second criterion is that the organization be *democratic*, i.e., that it be run in such a way that meaningful participation in decision-making is consistently available to each member (at least within his area of competence and concern) and that top decisions and decision-makers are ultimately accountable to and removable by the working membership.

3. Our final critierion applies a *humanistic* standard, which we defined to mean that the functioning of the organization not be at the expense of its members, fundamentally alienating them, consistently manipulating them, or dehumanizing them and that it not subordinate them to the status of material factors (Fibich, 1967).

The first criterion contains one reason why the model possesses several cybernetic characteristics—we have required it to be an on-going, self-steering system. The criterion of democracy indicates how the self-steering should take place. It thus reduces the number of possible forms of management that could fill the model, even though some excluded forms might be cybernetically and economically viable, such as the conventional corporation.

The humanistic criterion was actually accepted later in the development of our research, held off at first for fear of its being too vague or too broad. But we discovered that to specify as precisely as possible the democratic criterion it was necessary to apply the further criterion of humanism, or more exactly, humanization, as we now conceive it. For even democratic structures can contain certain possibilities for covert manipulation, leading to "pseudo-participation" (Pateman, 1970:69–71). Moreover, the evidence from Yugoslavia that serious alienation (not just momentary disaffection) is experienced by some members of workers' councils suggests that the democratic criterion by itself is insufficient to distinguish qualitatively the fully democratized institution (Obradovic, 1970).

With these criteria guiding the selection, six components have emerged so far which, working together, satisfy the stipulated conditions. If any one of the six is not present in empirical cases then the democratization decays, evidence has shown, or a crisis occurs demanding establishment of the missing component(s). The six minimally necessary components are as follows:

1. Participation in decision-making, whether direct or by elected representation. (Though this requirement seems obvious there are schemes calling themselves "economic democratization"—such as profit-sharing—which have not included participation in decision-making.)
2. Frequent feedback of economic results to all employees (in the form of money, not just information).
3. Full sharing with employees of management-level information and, to an increasing extent, management-level expertise.
4. Guaranteed individual rights (corresponding, it turns out, to the basic political liberties).
5. An independent board of appeal in case of disputes (composed of peers as far as possible).
6. A particular set of attitudes and values (type of consciousness).

LIMITATIONS

The model does not claim to cover all conditions pertaining to democratization; it focuses only on internal factors. The internal region proved sufficiently complex that to attempt more in one study did not seem prudent.

Although democratization of the workplace encompasses political, economic, and psychological phenomena, we have concentrated mostly on the political; that is, we focussed on questions of authority, decision-making, worker and management rights, and access to power. Psychological categories came into play insofar as the employees' motivation to participate emerged as a major linkage between the components. As that willingness to participate varies, the character of the entire self-governing system varies.

Basic economic issues such as capitalization of the firm, expansion, and diversification of product line are only touched upon in the present work. (For intensive treatment of them elsewhere see Vanek, 1972a, 1972b; Flaes, 1974). On the other hand, economic matters which play a more immediate role in the worker's life, such as wages and division of the profits, receive more attention here. And economic factors which function as external pressures on the firm's profitability we incorporated as a basic parameter of the model, requiring the internal components to accomodate their functioning to these environmental constraints.

A further limitation of the present study is that it does not treat technical factors of the work-process. Although technical factors can be influential at certain levels of democratization, our case data did not show them to outweigh other general factors facilitating or preventing democratization over its entire range.

Part I

EMPIRICAL CASES OF
WORKPLACE DEMOCRATIZATION

2

Advanced Democratization
In the American Plywood Industry

Eighteen plywood manufacturing firms in Oregon and Washington are fully owned by their employees and to varying degrees, are also managed by them.*

These companies make up about one-eighth of the American plywood industry. They range in size from 80 to 450 owner-workers and in gross annual earnings from $3 million to $15 million (Poor's, 1974; Berman, 1967; Bellas, 1972). They range from nineteen to thirty-three years of continuous operation.

Two scholarly works describe the history of the firms and their management process (Berman, 1967; Bellas, 1972). For the present research seven firms were selected for on-site investigation, as representative of the total population of eighteen, considering the variables of age, size, conditions of origin, legal category of incorporation, urban/rural location, and economic performance. In autumn 1973, in-depth interviews were conducted with leading management personnel, workers' elected representatives, and rank-and-file members. The questions posed were of an exploratory nature, and a promise of anonymity in reporting them was a condition of access. The report that follows draws on the two earlier published works as well as the data gained through these interviews.

FOUNDING OF WORKER-OWNED FIRMS

The first such company, Olympia Plywood, was founded in 1921 (Berman, 1967:85). A group of lumbermen, carpenters, and mechanics pooled their resources and built a plant by their own labor in Olympia, Washington. Most of the workers were heirs to a Scandinavian tradition of cooperative enterprise, common to that immigrant population of the Pacific Northwest. To assemble the materials and to purchase a site, the

---

*In Washington these companies are (name in italics equals the company and the town): Buffelen Woodworking Company in Tacoma; *Elma* Plywood Corporation; *Everett* Plywood Corporation; *Fort Vancouver* Plywood Company; Hardell Mutual Plywood Corporation in Olympia; *Hoquiam* Plywood Company; *Lacey* Plywood Company; Mt. Baker Plywood, Inc. in Bellingham; North Pacific Plywood, Inc. in Tacoma; *Stevenson* Co-Ply, Inc.; and Puget Sound Plywood, Inc., in Tacoma. In Oregon: *Astoria* Plywood Corporation; *Brookings* Plywood Corporation; Linnton Plywood Association in Portland; *Medford* Veneer and Plywood Corporation; *Milwaukie* Plywood Corporation; Multnomah Plywood Corporation, in Portland; and Western States Plywood Cooperative in Port Orford.

125 workmen had to contribute $1,000 each, which they raised by cashing in savings bonds, borrowing from friends, pledging future wages, or mortgaging personal property. In return for their individual contribution each worker received by contract a share in the new company entitling him to employment, an equal share in the profits, and an equal vote in directing all company affairs. The company commenced manufacture in August with workers electing a board of directors from their own number to manage affairs, although the whole body of workers frequently reassembled to receive information on the state of the enterprise and to set policy in matters that immediately affected them, such as pay. After the initial sacrifice, the company prospered. Plywood was then a relatively new industry with a steadily increasing demand, and Olympia quickly developed a reputation for high-quality products (Berman, 1967: 85–92). Three other worker-owned companies were established just before World War II in much the same way. (Anacortes, Veneer, Inc., Peninsula Plywood Corp., in Port Angeles; and Puget Sound Plywood, all in Washington state.) They, too, found a ready market for plywood, which was being further boosted by wartime demand.

A few years after the war a private plywood company became the frist to convert to worker-ownership. As the market price of plywood was then declining and there were problems getting logs, the owner of Oregon-Washington Plywood Co. in Tacoma decided to sell his business. A few workers in this firm were aware of the four successful worker-owned mills and began a campaign to convince their fellow employees to buy the company. Though raising the money would be a hardship and the project itself risky, about three-fifths of the firm's employees pledged their support. The original owner not only agreed to the arrangement, but even offered to stay on as sales broker for the first six months.

Again, $1,000 was the sum set for each man to contribute. Since more than twice that amount was needed to buy the company, each worker bought a second share on time. The new shareowners also decided to lower their wages to create operating capital for the first few months. The market price of plywood continued to decline during that first year, and the going was rough. But the men worked hard and were willing to defer payment of part of their wages. The next year brought a boom market for plywood, and the company, renamed North-Pacific Plywood, Inc., has prospered ever since.

Indeed, the ability of worker-owned mills to survive the severe price-swings characteristic of the plywood market helped lead to the creation of over twenty worker-owned companies by the mid-fifties. Shares of the prewar firms had risen in value from the initial $1,000 to $40,000 or $50,000 and this gave other workers more confidence in their ability to buy and successfully operate closed or bankrupt conventional firms. Some nonworkers became attracted to the idea too, and a curious new breed of business promoter cropped up. These promoters arranged the establishment of worker-owned companies, taking a cut of the profits as their service fee. Some of the agent-created companies quickly failed, and a few agents were taken to court for fraud. The resulting scandal somewhat cooled local ardor for launching any more worker-owned firms. After 1955, none seem to have been founded (Berman, 1967: 113–116).

SYSTEM OF SELF-GOVERNMENT

The organization of the plants varies from one to another, but all reflect the same general process. Employee-shareholders meet annually to elect from their own number a board of directors (which could just as accurately be termed a workers' council). The board makes most policy decisions, but its power is checked by the whole group; for example, expenditures over $25,000 must be approved by the entire membership of the company. Similarly, any major decision to invest, build a subsidiary plant, borrow a large sum of money, open a sales contract, or sell a sizable asset must be voted on by all the workers. In some companies the rank-and-file can challenge a board decision by collecting a petition of 10 to 20 percent of the membership and calling a special shareholders' meeting to decide the issue.

A president, vice-president, and secretary-treasurer are also elected yearly. In several mills, the president is the worker who received the most votes in the board election. The elections themselves seem to be partly a popularity contest, partly the selection of genuine business-leadership talent, and partly an expression of task-group friendships. This last factor means there are representatives on the board from different parts of the productive process. This is true in many mills and is usually considered by managers to be an advantage. It gives them an accurate picture of opinion throughout the company and makes it easier to circulate information back to every task group. Also, managers expressed satisfaction in the interviews that this mechanism allows each group to learn directly from each other about problems of the plant, rather than having to be told by the managers themselves.

The board of directors appoints a general manager to coordinate day-to-day affairs. He is the company's expert on business matters and usually comes from outside the firm. The rest of the administrative staff consists of a plant supervisor, sales manager, logs purchaser, accountant, shipping expediter, and their assistants, usually all shareowners.

The governing process in the mills is based on a circular pattern of authority (see Figure 2.1). The workers hire the manager, set his salary, and make all major decisions on company expansion, modernization, diversification, and so forth. Yet on a day-to-day basis they work under the manager's direction. The directors, elected by their fellow workers, receive neither deference nor extra pay, and continue to work in the plant while serving on the board. Thus it becomes impossible for them to avoid suggestions from other workers. Several directors commented on the number of times they are "told off" by their fellow workers in the course of a week. Worker-owners feel free to walk into the general manager's office as well, with complaints or suggestions. If for some reason he is not

Figure 2.1 FLOWS OF AUTHORITY AND COMMUNICATION IN THE WORKER-MANAGED PLYWOOD FIRMS

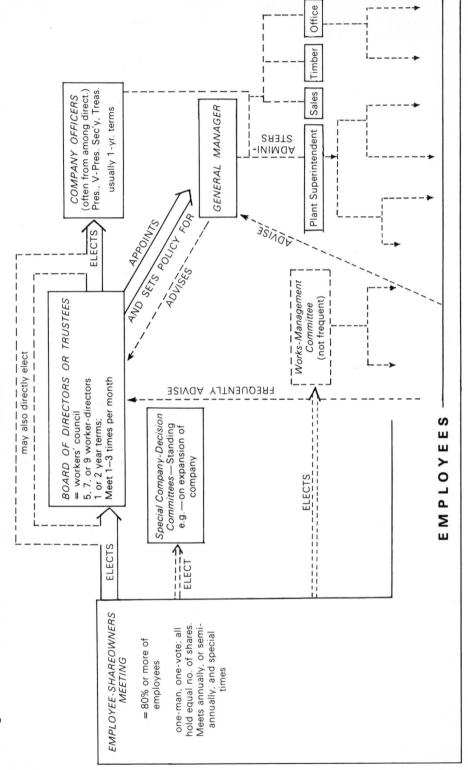

EMPLOYEES

available, they can ask the company president, a fellow worker, to speak to the manager for them. In contrast to many political democracies, participation remains at a high level after elections.

Of course, some workers are more involved than others. These workers feel a strong responsibility to make the company succeed; they learn all they can about the company's problems; and they run for director. Others who are known to be talented refuse to take on leadership responsibility: "Why bother? It's too much of a hassle," is their attitude. A good number of workers feel incapable of being leaders and offer only a suggestion or two. Almost all, however, feel willing to complain to any director or officer. Finally, there are some worker-owners who do not participate at all. They consider their company to be like any other mill except that it provides more take-home pay.

On the whole, then, the worker-owned mills exhibit a gradation in participation and political maturity somewhat like that reported by political scientists for political democracies in general: a proportion of activists, a proportion of "occasionals," and a proportion of "apathetics" (R. Dahl, 1963: Ch. 6). But in these firms the "occasional" and "apathetic" categories seem much smaller than what has been reported about national politics, and the active participants' category seems significantly larger. Also, the flow of criticism upwards is strikingly greater in these mills, and the sense of alienation from top decisions that is common in regular politics is almost entirely absent.

To supplement the informal communication network where worker-directors talk with their friends back on the production line, company issues are presented to shareowners in more formal ways. In the most concerned companies, monthly reports are sent to each worker's home. These reports give the company's profit-and-loss statement, its output, inventory, sales situation, and other crucial economic transactions usually reserved for top executives in the standard corporation. In less diligent worker-owned firms, a shorter statement is prepared quarterly and left in a stack on a table for interested workers to pick up. Reports from the twice-monthly board meetings are posted in most companies. At year's end the company financial statement is circulated to all worker-owners, and in at least one firm, a complete audit is mailed to each member, revealing exactly what has been paid to every other member of the firm.

Members told this researcher they had no trouble being prepared for a general shareholders' meeting. Even if the agenda were not printed up, everyone knew what matters were at hand. "Regular talk in the plant *is* about the company," they reported.

Much of the success or failure of the worker-owned mill depends upon the general manager. He needs both sound business sense and the ability to present his viewpoint convincingly to the directors. His relationship with the members affects their motivation in the mill as workers. It also affects their flexibility and wisdom in making long-run business decisions as owners.

Many a manager has found himself caught between the workers' wants and his own judgment of what is best for the firm. He must deal with a basic tension between the workers' interests as wage-earners and their interests as owners. The first interest focuses on the short-run: "Give me my income now—as big a share of this year's surplus as possible." The other interest is long-term; for example: "We must reserve fifty to sixty percent of this year's surplus to purchase timberland so we'll have an assured supply of raw material in years to come."

Another tension exists between the workers' expertise about their specific jobs in the plant and their minimal knowledge about outside factors to be considered in collective decisions. Generally, leaders' complaints reflected this particular contradiction of interests:

> "It's hard to follow good business practice in this company. The share-owners take a limited approach to things."
> "Our firm needs to learn how good businesses can grow. Expansion is virtually nil in most worker-owned mills. The men want to work with what's closest to them. For instance, they've never entertained the thought of going beyond plywood (into other wood products)."
> "The men are too conservative about going into debt. They resist borrowing funds for plant improvement even after they agree that the upgrading should be done. They'd rather wait until we had enough cash on hand to pay for it."
> "The workers need to learn the value of risk-taking."

Two methods are relied upon to solve this problem. One is for the manager to show the workers clearly how their short-term interests depend on the firm's long-run investment. The other is to have many workers learn the facts of business directly by becoming directors. "I think every worker should be elected to the board at least once," remarked on old man in overalls, working by a board conveyor. "I was a director once, and really learned the problems of the company." A manager agrees: "There's a tremendous increase in the individual worker's understanding of business just from serving on the board."

PRODUCTIVITY

In spite of such difficulties the firms prosper. Evidently, considerable forces of productivity are released by the self-management process which can outweight the inefficiencies of semi-amateur management. Worker-owned mills have demonstrated their higher productivity compared to conventionally owned firms in the following ways:

1. Workers' collectives have many times taken bankrupt or losing private plywood firms and converted them into successful enterprises (Berman, 1967: 118–121).

2. Worker-owned firms' output averaged 115–120 square feet of plywood per man-hour in contrast to conventional firms' 80–95 square feet, during the 1950s (H. Dahl, 1957; cited by Berman, 1967: 189). During the 1960s, they were producing 170 square feet per man-hour compared to 130 square feet for conventional firms (Berman, 1967: 189–190).*

---

*Berman cautions against relying too heavily on output-per-man-hour figures, however, because the consensus in the plywood industry is that too many variables

3. When worker-owned firms were challenged by the Internal Revenue Service for paying their members higher than industry-level wages and for deducting those as labor costs, the companies were able to demonstrate to the satisfaction of the IRS auditor and the tax court judges that these higher wages were justified by their workers' 25 to 60 percent greater productivity than the plywood industry's average (Interview data; and Berman, 1967: 189–190).

4. In general, worker-owned mills operate at a higher percentage of capacity than do conventional mills (Berman, 1967: 94).

5. Whenever the entire industry has suffered from a slump in demand and private firms have thus had to lay off workers, worker-owned firms have been able to keep their men on the job. (They have thereby added to "social productivity" also, by saving state agencies or the community the burden of paying out unemployment compensation, and by sparing their workers' families the interpersonal problems that can accompany unemployment).

Motivations behind this greater productivity are apparent in the attitudes of members, as expressed in these comments:

> "When the mill is your own, you really work hard to make a go of it."
> "Everyone digs right in—and wants the others to do the same. If they see anybody trying to get a free ride, they get on his back right quick."
> "Group pressure here is more powerful than any foreman could be."
> "If a guy held back, he didn't feel right. Actually, he was stealing from the others."

Thus pride of ownership motivates the majority to produce more than hired workers, and mutual supervision keeps potential laggards from lowering the standard.

The effect of the self-management system on supervision and productivity is demonstrated by the experience of a firm whose worker-owners recently sold their company to a large conglomerate. (The reasons for that sale are discussed later.) Under the new owner, eight more foremen are needed, though there are 100 fewer workers. The plant superintendent, who had worked under both systems, was asked if there were any differences now that the firm was no longer worker-owned:

> "Oh, certainly, people were eager then. They were more efficient. You could depend on them to stay often beyond five o'clock. Nobody worried about time—their aim was just to finish the product."

The workers expressed similar feelings:

> "Before, a guy took real pride in his work. Now we come just for the money."
> "The men used to boast about their output. Now no one cares."

---

affect that measure. Nevertheless, the consistency of the difference in output between self-managed and private firms over several years and across many firms cannot be ignored.

EARNINGS

Because their roots are in a cooperative, egalitarian philosophy, the plywood mills pay all members an equal wage: floorsweeper, skilled panel-finisher, and accountant alike. Since certain jobs may take longer than others, or a machine may be shut down for repairs and put someone off work for a few hours, a sophisticated system of record-keeping has evolved to equalize the final take-home pay. Every week or month a person's hours at work are totaled and whoever has less than the standard is given first bid for weekend work to bring his total pay up to equality. He need not actually work then if he prefers not to, but he must be offered the opportunity. Likewise, those whose weekly or monthly totals exceed that period's standard must reduce their hours during the next period to the level which allows for equal income.

Highly skilled workers sometimes resent not receiving more pay than men who do the simplest jobs in the firm. And some members regard equal wages as unrealistic, especially because in low-profit years a few workers may leave the company for higher paying jobs elsewhere. (In those years the fixed wage of the highest union-scale job in other plants may be better than the variable wage in a hard-hit worker-owned mill.) In order not to lose men in bad years from certain crucial jobs such as electrician or mechanic, some firms have made these into nonowner positions. Men are hired for those posts at higher salaries than the egalitarian pay. However, most worker-owners are reluctant to create hired, salaried jobs, so the practice is strictly limited to a few positions, most often the general manager.

During all but the worst market times, average pay is almost always higher in worker-owned plywood companies than in other firms, not only on an hourly basis (which usually averages twenty-five percent higher) but also because of the year-end division of the profits. The latter has run to several thousand dollars per person in good years. Sometimes a portion of the bonus is retained in a pension fund, managed by a bank to increase its value. Sometimes a portion is converted into "Finance Fund Certificates." (These certificates are used by the company to generate significant amounts of capital, in effect borrowing from its worker-owners. The certificates are redeemable within three to ten years, paying four to eight percent interest.) And finally, each worker receives the full value of his share when he leaves the company, either by selling it to an incoming worker or to the company itself. Such shares typically bring $20,000 to $40,000.

There are other material benefits as well for worker-owners, which vary somewhat from firm to firm: free lunches in the company's own restaurant; full medical care, including dental and eye care, and coverage for each family; the workers' own gasoline supply at wholesale prices; and company-paid life insurance. All of these fringe benefits were obtained years before unions were able to secure just a few of them for workers in regular plywood mills.

Cooperation in these firms includes the freedom to take time off when needed. From one day to three months can be requested in addition to the worker's paid vacation. The requests are usually granted because the flexibility of work assignments in the firm allows other workers to take over the missing person's responsibilities. The only restriction is that he not use his time off for moonlighting because then he would be violating one basic obligation of his stock-ownership: to contribute equal labor to the common enterprise.

One complaint in the firms is that the older workers do not, in effect, live up to this obligation because they are kept on beyond their usefulness to the company. Retirement is not compulsory, and the employment of older members who are less efficient is criticized by some as a form of featherbedding. Of course, one might regard the employment of older workers who want to continue working to be far more humane than the forced retirement characteristic of conventional companies. Workers in the plywood firms can continue their life-long trade among close friends during their last years instead of being forced into involuntary idleness.

THE NON-OWNING WORKER

In addition to using one or two highly paid, nonowning, skilled workers, many mills employ ordinary production workers on a much larger scale. This practice seems contrary to their egalitarian philosophy. The number of these nonowning workers varies from season to season and from firm to firm. It can be as high as a third of a mill's workforce, but most often it is around 10 or 15 percent. Some of the hired employees are sons or sons-in-law of current shareowners, interested in temporary employment during the vacation months and not in ownership. A few others were considered too old when they joined to be able to complete payments on a share before retirement. Others are temporary workers hired during peak-demand seasons, who then stay with the company for years if the sales level stays higher than when they were first hired.

The most basic reason nonowning workers are not brought in as equal partners is that shareowners fear their own stock must be devalued in order to add more shareowners to the fixed asset-value of the firm. (Of course, high demand for a job at the mill can drive the price higher than that minimum value, which accounts for the prices cited earlier.) "You'd be cutting the melon into thinner slices," explained one worker. For this reason worker-owners prefer to let a new person purchase a share only when a current member leaves. A second major reason for the accumulation of nonowning workers is that sometimes, even when a share is available, a job-seeker cannot afford it. A down payment of $2,000 at least is normally required, and there is a monthly deduction from wages to complete the purchase of a share. These installments can run $150 to $250 per month for up to ten years.

A third group of nonowning workers are hired on at special plants at forest sites. At these plants logs are cut into thin sheets of veneer, the first step in plywood manufacture. Worker-owned companies seem always to have treated their veneer plants as subsidiaries, never having opted for multiple-plant democracy or for a federation of self-governing plants. A few shareowners are stationed at these forest mills as supervisors, but the remainder of the workforce are hired hands.

Non-owning employees at the plywood companies do not receive the same fixed, egalitarian wage as shareowners; they are paid according to the prevailing industry-wide union scale. However, they usually enjoy the same fringe benefits as shareowners: paid holidays, life insurance, medical plans, and a Christmas bonus. And they have the same physical working conditions. Nevertheless, they cannot participate in any of the firm's self-government. The other workers are their bosses, not partners, and usually they are not protected by a union.

UNIONS

Nonowning workers do benefit indirectly from union gains achieved in conventional plants, for the rule of thumb seems to be to give them at least what the industry-wide union contract requires. Two unions represent almost all workers in the plywood industry, the International Woodworkers of America [CIO] and the Lumber and Sawmill Workers Union [AFL]. Contracts are negotiated with an association of private company owners called the Timber Operators Council. In one large mill, which regularly employs about 100 nonowning workers (one quarter of the total workforce), the men did belong to a union which represented them to the board of directors. More details are still needed about union organizing in other worker-owned mills. The few nonowning workers encountered during the course of this investigation seemed unconcerned. One worker said that he did "miss the backing" he had enjoyed as a union member in a private firm.

Interestingly, union officials generally take a dim view of the worker-owned mills, even those without hired men. When the plywood market is severely depressed and worker-owned mills lower their pay to shareowners, the unions fear this could threaten the wage scale they have achieved in conventional mills. (In fact, the latter has not led to any lowering of the union scale by private owners.)

The attitude of most worker-owners toward the unions is dormantly sympathetic. They had been union members before they founded their own companies and many keep up their union membership. But they are not active as a local union chapter because the main function of their union, negotiating for higher wages and better working conditions, is something they take care of themselves.

The situation is fundamentally anomolous. But the anomaly is resolved once we understand worker-owned mills as a *third system:* neither capitalist ownership, nor its counterforce, the union-organized labor pool. Unions came into being because capitalists existed; that is, given that company decision-making power was first reserved to the holders of capital, unions sprang up to try to wrest away some of that power, to place it into the hands of the other members of the company—laborers. However, when a company exists whose laborers are already the holders of capital, the original abrogation of decision-making power has not been made. A union actually has little function to perform for them. However, a different conclusion is reached in conditions where ownership is in *state* hands, or where the democratization available to workers is only partial. There unions can have a vital role to play (Remington, 1969: 115; Gorz, 1967; Hunnius, 1973).

PROBLEMS OF CONTINUITY

At least twenty-six worker-owned mills have been in operation, but today there are only eighteen.* What happened to the others?

Two failed economically, one because the former parent company reneged on its agreement to set up a national sales organization for the fledgling enterprise. Another relied too heavily on a self-aggrandizing general manager, and by the time the worker-directors realized what he was doing, they were unable to rescue the firm from bankruptcy (Berman, 1967: 123–124).

Aside from economic failures, there are three or four worker-owned firms whose demise was caused ironically by their economic success. These firms continue as prosperous plywood mills but are no longer self-managed. Their worker-owners, nearing retiring age, sold their firms to conglomerates, to convert their individual share values into cash, and as a result transformed their cooperatives into standard corporations.

Successful firms are the most vulnerable to this, because their high value keeps the price of their shares high, out of the reach of most workers seeking employment yet within the range of big corporations who can offer to purchase many shares at once. This may be the only effective offer received by the members in a long time. Thus, wealthy conglomerates like ITT and the Times-Mirror Corporation have been attracted by the success of prosperous plywood firms and have made offers as high as $100,000 for each individual worker's share.

Even in companies where a majority of shareowners are not ready to retire, there may be incentives to accept a corporate offer. The higher price of shares in successful companies often means that each individual who does buy in must take a longer time to complete payment on his share. When a large number of shareowners are on such time-payments, they may see a generous takeover offer as an opportunity to be relieved of further payments and even to make a substantial profit. When this "unpaid-up" faction is added to those nearing retirement, a majority of shareowners may wish to accept a conglomerate's offer. A third factor in workers' decisions is the fluctuating price of plywood; for example, both Anacortes and Peninsula were sold after the two-year slump of 1967–1968 had put real hardships on the worker-owners. Thus, three of the oldest and most successful worker-owned mills have sold out to larger corporations (in 1954, 1969, and 1970). The life-span of each was about thirty years.

Despite their general laxity about corporate takeovers, the worker-

---

*The eight that have ceased operation and were not listed at the beginning of this chapter are: In Washington: *Olympia* Veneer Company (1921–1954); *Anacortes* Veneer, Inc. (1939–1969); Peninsula Plywood Corporation in Port Angeles (1941–1970); *Centralia* Plywood, Inc. (1951–1968); and Washington Plywood Company in Lowell (1955–1965). In California: Standard Veneer and Timber Company (1954–1971) and Northern California Plywood, Inc. (1954–1967) both in Crescent City; and Mutual Plywood Corporation in Eureka (1950–1958). Our study included interviews with members of two of these demised firms. See also Berman (1967:93, passim), who mentions the possibility of seven more such ventures which are no longer operating.

owned mills have given careful attention to ensuring their continuity insofar as sale of shares to individuals is concerned. In all the firms it is a basic rule that the company has first option to buy the share when an individual member decides to sell. If the company declines the option and the member finds a buyer, the board of directors still has the right to veto the new person. "After all," one president explained, "we're not just hiring; we're taking on a new partner."

Additionally, most companies have an informal trial period for new members. They are taken around the plant to work at various jobs alongside as many shareholders as possible. Some firms also put great store in having prospective members "sponsored," by being a friend or relative of a current (or outgoing) member. In firms that are not very careful in their selection procedures, one heard complaints about the younger generation: "They're not hard workers. They've grown up in the affluent era and don't have the same attitudes about the value of work." Younger people who were hard-working, however, were quickly recognized and respected.

The foregoing remarks refer only to the continuity of existing firms. There is also the issue of the continuity of the worker-owned mills as a group. Why have no new firms been added since the mid-1950s? One reason is that to start a new mill has become economically more difficult. The price of plywood is no longer steadily rising; instead, it cycles drastically. Over the same period the cost of the raw material, timber logs, has soared, and other employment has become available in the area (in particular, the aerospace and electronics industries). No longer are there community leaders or business agents offering to organize worker-owned mills. And perhaps the present generation is less willing than the past one to sacrifice a decent income during the two to four years of hardship usually required to get a self-managed mill fully underway.

Although there are a few leaders in these mills who express a desire to see their form of self-management spread, most worker-owners view their company not as a specimen of self-government to be preserved for its own sake, but primarily as a means for their own livelihood. There have been one or two instances of a new worker-owned mill spinning off from a parent collective (Berman, 1967: 238), but no general procedure has been developed by the worker-owned mills for significant proliferation.

A few efforts at joint activity have been undertaken. The most long-lived is a joint marketing association that includes Lacey, Hoquiam, Stevenson, Linnton, and North-Pacific plywood companies. The original intention was to include all the worker-owned mills and perhaps to corner the market on highly finished plywood, a product in which they excel. But antitrust laws set limits on the possibilities of official coordination, and not all sales managers and directors were committeed to helping the less successful firms. At the moment, some member mills are considering joint purchase of raw materials.

IMPLICATIONS

The unique experience of these worker-managed firms in America has made evident valuable possibilities for advanced democratization of the workplace:

1. The invention of the "working share," which secures for each person the rights of ownership, labor, and self-government, and does so on an egalitarian basis.
2. The existence already within the present legal environment of a space for workers' self-management: within state law through incorporation either as a cooperative or as a jointly-held corporation, and within federal law, after a series of battles with the Internal Revenue Service to define a mutually acceptable status under the tax laws.
3. The creation of a "workers' council" structure and process in the United States without the prelude of a socialist revolution and without waiting for a supportive change in labor union ideology.
4. Development of a mechanism to equalize the distribution of incomes between managing and working classes, again without waiting for government compulsion.
5. At the same time, the equalization of income was not gained at expense of lessening employee motivation or productivity, as other incentives were generated which yielded equal or greater output.

The founding and first years of these plywood companies offer general lessons as well, for the establishment of worker-owned companies in non-socialist environments:

Timing

Workers seem most willing to depart from the prevailing system and launch into self-management when the traditional system is obviously failing them. A good proportion of the mills were founded either during the Depression or when workers in a private mill saw their own employers about to close shop. The same was true for the Lip watch workers recently in France, an English leather goods factory, and the original Scanlon participation plan at Adamson Storage Tank Company in Ohio (Herman, 1974; Kasindorf, 1973; Lesieur, 1958). When closures are imminent and management is already relinquishing its power, there is no need for workers to force it out or coerce it into sharing power by a strike.

Economic Attributes

One major reason self-management was able to succeed in the plywood industry is that the manufacturing process is labor intensive and requires relatively low levels of capital. The capital required was within the range of what a group of highly motivated workers could assemble. A lot of the machinery they could even construct themselves. This offers a clue toward distinguishing which industries offer greater probabilities of success for the launching of worker-owned enterprises today (e.g., perhaps service sector and retail trades).

Another economic fact important to the establishment of self-manage-ment in plywood was that the earliest collectives began when the market was first developing. Market entry is a crucial factor in the fate of any enterprise, and the lesson implied by these mills is that persons interested in launching a worker-managed firm would do well to select as their product one whose market is still young and has plenty of potential for expansion.

Size

Manufacturing plywood does not require teams larger than are feasible for direct self-government. Apparently a self-governing manufacturing unit cannot go much above 350–400 members without encountering serious discontinuities of communication, interpersonal knowledge, interac-tion, etc. Larger collectives that aim for self-government usually find they have to segment themselves into units of this size or smaller, and then send delegates from each unit to a coordinating council. This is how self-manage-ment in gigantic industries has operated in East Europe (Hunnius, 1973; Stradal, 1969: 30–33).

No woker-managed plywood company ever grew to the size of the industry's giants (firms like Georgia-Pacific, Weyerhauser, and Crown-Zellerbach), even though worker-owned mills have been in the industry from its early years. However, they have survived the competition of these larger firms partly because an industry-wide association took on some of the research, development, and quality-control tasks which giants competing in many other industries usually fund by themselves. This organization, the American Plywood Association, is composed of both private and worker-owned firms and was by no means established to help worker-owned firms as a group. Nevertheless, its cooperative use of resources may be taken as one model of a mechanism to enable small production units to be econo-mically feasible in the modern economy. Also, some plywood firms were relieved of the burden of operating a sales-distribution network because a larger firm regularly bought all their output.

These two patterns suggest that whenever production can be carried out in small self-managed units, larger-scale, nonproduction activities such as sales and research might be assigned to a separate organization that would service the self-managed units.

In the next chapter we move to Europe and across the wide range of degrees of democratization. These companies were not founded by workers but began to be democratized gradually on the initiative of their private owners. In many cases, therefore, the degree of democratization achieved has not been as great as that experienced in the plywood firms and this leads us to several crucial discoveries.

Partial to Advanced Democratization: Illustrating the Range of Cases

To develop a model that would satisfy the requirements of breadth and flexibility, it was necessary, of course, to examine more than one type of democratization. Here we present a few different cases to illustrate the range of democratization that exists in autonomous firms—the range of cases from which we ultimately derived the model presented in Part II. Since it is not possible nor sensible to present in detail all the cases we examined (which are listed in Table 1.1) only a few selected cases, representative of distinctly different types of democratization, are discussed here. They illustrate how the essential components for the general model were uncovered. Then, in Part II, we shall draw on the remainder of our cases to fill out and refine the model.

Certain cases are called "partial" systems, because they usually allow the employees only partial control over the decisions that affect them. Nevertheless, these cases can be a valuable source of knowledge about democratization. The presence in each company of only one or two elements of democratization allows us to trace the consequences of each of these elements without the additional complexity of other components. Partial cases can, therefore, be analyzed in comparative perspective as a series of "natural experiments" (Babbie, 1975: 251—256). Furthermore, their resemblance to conventional enterprises on some dimensions helps us to discern what uniquely pertains to democratization. They challenge us to determine the boundary between democratized and non-democratized situations. Some of them, such as the Scanlon Plan, are very puzzling borderline cases, lacking worker-ownership but exhibiting much worker influence and a guaranteed employee share in profits. When taken together, therefore, these partial cases compel us to refine our concepts in order that they may accommodate the real achievements as well as the shortcomings of these cases. They thus help us to identify what is essential to democratization, though as cases they have perhaps been underplayed in much of the literature.

AN EARLY EXPERIENCE OF SELF-MANAGEMENT IN PRIVATE ENTERPRISE: THE BAT'A BOOT & SHOE CO.

In 1922, Thomas Bat'a, owner of several shoe factories in central Czechoslovakia, inaugurated a system of partial self-management in his plants (Dubreuil, 1963; ILO, 1930, Sprague, 1932, Cekota, 1964). Like much of Europe, Czechoslovakia was then caught in a serious recession, inflation was rampant, unemployment was speedily increasing. Bat'a's own firm had been suffering under huge debts incurred from its take-over during World War I by the Austro-Hungarian Army and from a huge warehouse fire one year after the war which had destroyed a major portion of his raw materials stocks. Now sales were declining because of the widespread unemployment and the general inflation. Instead of laying off his workers to cut costs in the short run, or raising prices as most other sellers were doing in a short-range attempt to increase revenue, Bat'a decided to *cut* the selling price of his product by almost half (46 percent), and to lower wages and salaries of all, including management, by 40 percent. To make up the difference and earn enough to stay in business, he resolved to reduce as far as possible the company's internal costs and waste by turning over responsibility increasingly to the employees.

Starting first on a pilot basis with forty-five workers, Bat'a formed them into a self-contained production unit. He gave the members of this unit full details on the costs of each activity they performed and every material that contributed to their production of shoes and boots. Imparting such information to one's workers was unique in industry at the time and remains rare even today. Yet we will see that it is indispensable to democratization* and even to the partial goal of repeatedly cutting the costs of production and improving productivity. Along with this information the workers received responsibility for losses and profits incurred by their unit, which were calculated from cost of their materials, power, labor, and plant maintenance in contrast with the sales value of the boots and shoes they turned out. Bat'a allowed his workers a 10 percent markup above production cost as the selling price for their output, and any increases in efficiency they achieved to lower the production cost while maintaining quality was returned to them as self-earned profit. Likewise, this team of workmen was held responsible for decreases in efficiency that raised the total cost of production without increasing quality. The workers kept accounts of every operation and its cost on a daily and weekly basis, so that any decline in efficiency would quickly alert them to re-examine their system of operations and to search for the fault—be it technical, psychological, or economic—as soon as possible.

The company provided the men with all necessary raw materials, tools, etc., and handled the sales of the finished product. Each worker was paid a basic wage but now the margin of return to the shop as a result of its own improvements in efficiency became an additional source of pay. At first the additional margin was divided 50 percent for the company and 50 percent to the self-administered workshop. Within the shop, 10 percent of the margin was distributed to the chief foreman, 2 percent to each keyman, and 1 percent to every participant worker. Persons whose jobs "had no decisive influence on the economy or quality of the work" received just the basic wage (Cekota, 1964:342–349).

After the successful operation of this test scheme, Bat'a eventually re-organized the rest of his workers, and the production of shoes by the company soared. The original halving of price had caused a first surge in

---

*See chapter 6, below.

sales, for even in recession times people need shoes. The new method of self-management proved extraordinarily successful in supplying the increased consumer demand. Just the next year Bat'a was able to lower prices by one-sixth (about 17 percent) and to *raise* wages 25 percent. He than began to extend self-administration to all other areas of company operations: accounting, ordering, finance, sales, etc. Workshops were grouped into lots, and lots into semi-independent confederations, all self-administered. Every six months each unit worked out a detailed plan of production, distribution, sales, costs, and profits and made this plan the standard by which their weekly performance was to be assessed (Hindus, 1947: 74).

By 1926, only four years after inception of the plan, wages to workers in the Bat'a company had risen on the average 44 percent, while the average price of shoes to the customer had been lowered by just over 40 percent (beyond the initial slashing of prices in half). In the meantime, the workshops' share of profit had been raised from 50 percent to 80 percent, the company now receiving only 20 percent. The following year conveyor production was installed, so the continued success of the company after that time must be understood as a mixture of technical innovations and the self-administration system. By 1931, when serious worldwide economic depression was affecting Czechoslovakia, the Bat'a company was paying its workers 310 percent of their original (1922) wage, yet charging its customers only 39 percent the original price. Furthermore, the workshops' share in profits had been increased to 98 percent. In addition, the company had been able to increase its daily production of shoes from 7,000 pairs in 1922 to 142,000 in 1931 (Cekota, 1964). Seven years later production had risen further to 180,000 pairs with several plants in foreign countries as well as some new ones in Czechoslovakia, and Bat'a output included hosiery, chemicals, books, machine tools, woodwork, bricks, cardboard, textiles, leather tanning, rubber tires, and airplanes (Hindus, 1947: 69–70; Cekota, 1964).

Although the success of this company is quite impressive, some qualifications are required from the viewpoint of our interest in democratization. Though the workshops did receive considerable autonomy, the workers did not actually choose their own managers, but rather worked together to achieve a common goal with managers appointed from their own ranks by Bat'a or one of his few aides (ILO, 1930: 236–238). Thus his system was not one of total self-management but rather a highly developed and refined system of self-administration. That means decisions on company-wide policy were still made by the owner—and could be made by him at any level whenever he wished. But most decisions involving the application of his policies in the detailed and day-to-day areas of business were made by the autonomous workshop teams. The company was highly *decentralized*, therefore, but not fully *democratized*. It lacked a system of workers' representation; i.e., spokesmen who have been elected by the workers and who authoritatively participate in decisions governing all policies of the company while still working at their regular jobs. On the other hand, Bat'a's was a pioneering effort in employee participation, it succeeded impressively during a severe period of European economic history, and it proved itself viable in many different countries and cultures—from Malaya to Canada and many lands in between. It included the important factor of earnings sharing, Additionally, some of the elements requisite in the ethos of democratized enterprises, such as cooperation and personal responsibility, were consciously encouraged in Bat'a's enterprises and in the schools of management he established to train workers for higher posts in the company (Sprague, 1932: 287–288). (See Chapters 5 and 9, below).

Besides Bat'a's own system, Czechoslovakia inaugurated two systems of workers' participation in management by national law in the early 1920s. One system applied to all private companies in the country that employed more than thirty persons; the other to all mining concerns with more than twenty workers. The miners' councils had more power than councils in other busines- ses, largely because their union had been the most strongly organized behind the demand for participation. There is not the space to present this case in detail, but we shall draw upon one of its innovations in our discussion of the adjudication of participants' rights (chapter 8). A detailed description of it is found in Bloss (1938: 135–140, 169) and further developments in Papanek (1946: 47), Hindus (1947: 190–193), and Kovanda (1974).

THE SCANLON PLAN IN AMERICA

For decades the most widespread *single* scheme of employee participa- tion in management in America has been the so-called Scanlon Plan. This system operates in at least fifty manufacturing firms, in industries as diverse as furniture manufacture, steel corrugated paper, silverware, radio and television manufacturing, rubber processing, and printing (Schultz, 1958: 55). In a step beyond the Bat'a system, the Scanlon Plan does employ a system of workers' representation. Two levels of committees are elected. The production committee in each department is composed jointly of representatives of management and a greater number of employees. At a higher level exists a single "screening committee" for the whole company. This is composed of top officers and high level managers of the firm (president or executive vice-president, treasurer, chief engineer, plant manager, etc.) and an equal number of employee representatives from the lower production committees, plus the local union president.

None of the workers' representatives possess formal voting power in these committee decisions, but formal voting has not appeared necessary for workers' input to be successful in decades of experience with this system (Lesieur, 1958: 42–49). Since the plan is installed in each company only with the active desire of management and usually begins with an explicit memorandum of understanding drawn up by both sides, management's willingness to listen seriously has combined with the frequently high utility of employees' suggestions from their on-the-job experience to yield a 90 percent adoption record (Lesieur, 1958:49).

The job of production committees, however, is not to set policy, but only to gather and develop employee suggestions for improving any or all aspects of production. Management, for its part, brings to the committee meetings observations on problems anticipated in the next week's or month's production and workers present their suggestions on how to ease those problems, plus other suggestions from their previous experience. The minutes of these departmental meetings are forwarded to the single screening committee as soon as possible. There, the possible ramifications of each proposal on the company as a whole are considered. Suggestions which can be implemented at the department level and have already been agreed to there are recorded; suggestions already rejected there are reviewed; and issues about which no agreement could be reached in production committees are reconsidered and sometimes adopted.

It is important to realize that these committees of worker-representation have not replaced the union function in Scanlon Plan companies where unions were already present. Instead, the two types of labor organization observe a specialization of functions, the Scanlon committees keeping to matters of production and other company concerns (engineering, marketing, and so forth), the unions retaining their traditional role of bargaining on wages, fringe benefits, and physical working conditions (Lesieur, 1958: 83, 126,130). Discussions of democratization often overlook the fact that room is available for both unions and production committees (or even more elaborate forms of worker participation) in workplace relations. But this was articulated in the U.S. at least as early as 1921 (Douglas, 1921:102–107) and analyzed and explained in the European context many times (Jenkins, 1973: Remington, 1969:115).

After the representation system, the second fundamental element of the Scanlon Plan is the monthly calculation and payment of returns on productivity increases (Puckett, 1958:65–79). At the inception of the plan, a ratio is calculated between the average monthly output achieved by the firm (usually measured in dollar sales-value of product) and total payroll costs per month during the last several months the company operated at a profit. This ratio then becomes the standard against which each subsequent month's production is measured. Each time that ratio is exceeded a portion of the increase is distributed as a bonus to all members participating in the plan—whether worker or manager—in proportion to their normal wage or salary level. Thus, like the Bat'a system, increases in productivity which are the result of collective discussion and on-the-job effort are returned to the persons who actually caused the improvement, not kept in the company treasury or distributed just to stockholders as though the workers had nothing to do with the rise in productivity.

Through the Scanlon Plan the company can benefit from higher efficiency and lowered production costs (more produced from the same initial expenditure), individual workers can benefit from higher take-home pay (through the bonus), and stockholders can benefit because higher efficiency and output boosts total company profits and eventually dividends. Like the Bat'a system, no bonus can be paid in months where productivity has not increased. That lack of bonus alerts workers and managers alike to search for the cause of lowered productivity and to correct it as soon as possible. (To cover costs in months when productivity falls, one-fourth of each surplus-month's margin is put in reserve).

In the Scanlon system we see emphasized a feedback loop between participation in decision-making and economic reward from increases in productivity or profits produced by those participants. This feedback loop

emerged as crucial to successful democratization in other systems as well*
and was present even in the Bat'a system. When we examine more ambitious
forms of employee self-management, such as the following worker-owned
companies, a few other elements emerge as crucial. Indeed, if we return to
Scanlon, Bat'a, and other partial cases and search for these other elements,
we can discover most of them at work there too, contributing to the success
of those systems, but in a form too subtle to have stood out prominently on
first inspection or to have been highlighted by their original authors.

VARIETIES OF DEMOCRATIZATION UNDER
WORKER-OWNERSHIP

Like the plywood firms already described, the following three firms are
owned by their employees. Private stockholders cannot choose their management as was the case in Scanlon Plan companies. Nor does the state appoint
their management as is done in Soviet-type "workers' democracies." Instead,
these worker-owned firms are ruled with varying degrees of directness
by their employees, or rather—since all are employees and co-owners—by
their *members*. Thus these enterprises are not what normally is thought of
as capitalist, where those who own the capital of a company have ultimate
power over all others in the company. Neither are they Marxian socialist,
for their common ownership of the means of production was not achieved
through intervention of the state. Rather, all members of the company are
both proprietors and employees: they own what they work with and exercise
control over the fruits of their labor.

However, these firms are unlike the plywood companies in that they
were not founded by their workers but rather were initially private firms
owned by a single proprietor and his family. After years of conventional
operation, each firm was converted to worker-ownership at the initiative
of that original proprietor. The motivations for conversion had varied roots—
a Quaker background in the case of one owner; a fundamentalist, charitable
Christian background in the case of another; a working-class experience by
an aristocratic scion in a third case. These aspects of the origin of each
company's democratization system have colored its respective progress
to the present day, even though each company has gone through several
decades of democratization.

AN EMPLOYEE-OWNED CONGLOMERATE:
THE JOHN LEWIS PARTNERSHIP

John Lewis Partnership, Ltd., does an average yearly business of
£60 million (equivalent to $168 million), employs nearly 17,000 persons
("partners"), and consists of sixteen department stores (including the
Selfridges chain), thirty-two food and other retail shops, and several
household goods factories, comprising in all twenty-nine companies
(Farrow, 1964; Flanders et al., 1968 :33). The founder, John Spedan Lewis

---

*See chapter 5, below.

Figure 3.1

FLOWS OF AUTHORITY AND COMMUNICATION
IN THE JOHN LEWIS PARTNERSHIP

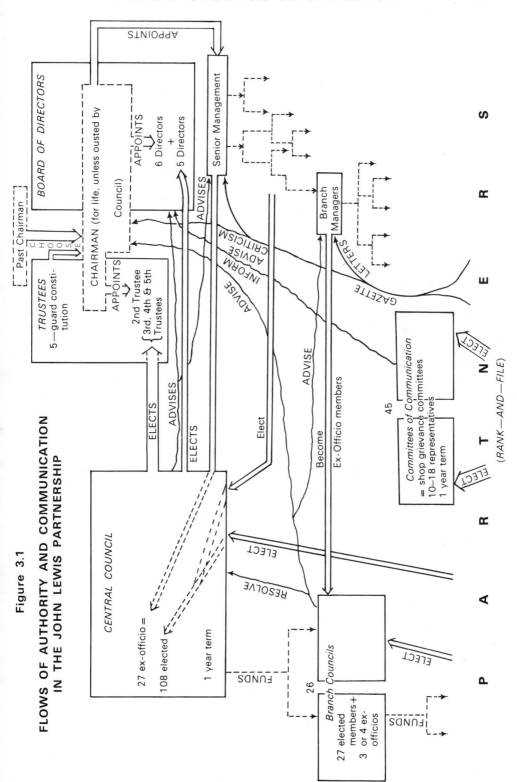

started with two stores inherited from his father in 1914. He had been shocked by the fact that his father was taking home from the business annually more than he paid all his other employees combined. Resolving to create a mechanism whereby the wealth an enterprise produces and the knowledge and power needed to run it might be shared more fairly, he turned over his growing chain of stores to its employees, present and future, beginning in 1929 with a transfer of stock to five trustees. Three of these are elected by an employee-chosen council (see Figure 3.1). The new "Partnership" reimbursed Lewis for the full monetary value of the shares by payments out of revenue over a twenty-year period. After 1950, then, the partnership was wholly employee-owned.

Members elect annually 108 representatives to a central council to which belong also about twenty-seven ex-officio members from the highest managing posts. The duties of this council are to rule on any proposal which could raise or lower the company's fixed assets by more than 5 percent (such as sale of a subsidiary or issue of a new series of loan certificates) and to recommend a policy line to senior management on any other issue brought to the council by a member. The council's recommendations are not binding on management, though they do have significant influence. The council also elects annually five of the twelve-man board of directors, the other six being chosen by the chairman. The chairman himself has been named by the previous chairman and trustees but takes office only with approval of the council. His post carries extensive powers—perhaps too extensive for an enterprise claiming to be democratic—and he is in office for life or until he chooses to retire, unless the council votes by a three-fourths majority that he has violated the constitution of the partnership and removes him. In this case the trustees of the constitution appoint the next chairman.

After 1940 when the partnership had expanded considerably, branch councils were established with similar advisory powers as the central council. The branch councils may make their formal recommendations to the branch manager or may go over his head to the senior management of the partnership, including the chairman. If still not satisfied, they may request the central council to take up their appeal and send its own recommendation on the matter to the chairman, directors, and senior management.

In addition, the central and branch councils decide on the expenditure of approximately $250,000 annually toward employees' and their families' welfare.

The bottom level of employee-representation at John Lewis is the committees of communication, which meet every second month with the partnership's chairman or his representative and function mostly as grievance committees. Their strength lies in bypassing the employees' immediate managers and communicating directly with the top, i.e., their managers' own bosses.

It can already be seen that the specific strategy for worker control over management at John Lewis relies on a many-channeled and, therefore, complex transmission of employee opinion upwards to each and every level of management. This is reinforced by an equally or even more complex system of checks and feedback *within* the structure of management itself, which unfortunately we do not have the space to present here (Flanders et al., 1968; ch. 10). Other self-owned companies have simpler systems of self-government (for instance, the plywood companies diagrammed in Figure 2.1) because they have granted the employee councils direct and binding power over most management decisions. These two different strategies are essentially poles of a single continuum, and any well-functioning democratized enterprise is likely to rely on a mixture of advisory consultations and binding, direct employee decision-making. John Lewis's system bears the mark of its chief designer, the founder of the partnership, who aimed not for selection of managers by the managed, but only for managers to be held accountable to the managed by their frequent expression of opinions. The model for Lewis was the British constitutional monarchy, not notions of workers' sovereignty or a model of direct democracy.

The final mechanism in the partnership's system to hold management accountable to the rest of the partners is a unique internal press. The weekly *Gazette* is an internal newsletter in which any partner may express criticism of any company official and demand a written response. For employee protection all criticism is published anonymously. If the official named or the one responsible for the matter under criticism is reluctant to reply, the employee may petition the trustees to order that manager to respond. In this way dissatisfaction may not become bottled up in a bureaucratic complaint department, remaining unknown to the rest of the company and ignored by those who are in a position to set the matter right. At the same time, however, there is no guarantee that the public complaint will be enough to correct the dissatisfying situation. The *Gazette* also serves as a means for circulating management-level knowledge to the rank-and-file, supplementary to the discussions in councils between ex-officios and elected representatives.

Besides the factors of circulation of information and representation of employees' will,* we notice two other factors in John Lewis that seem to be basic elements in its democratization: the protection of individual rights and an employee share in the profits.† To protect partners from arbitrary dismissal, the partnership relies on a division in management functions: an intercessor, "the Partner's Counselor," who possesses senior-management and can rank, can veto decisions of lower management against an employee. In addition, the councils can take an employee's side in a wage or dismissal matter in appeals to top management (though management still has the final say). Finally, partners are protected from retaliation against their opinion in the *Gazette* by the practice of anonymity and are protected in their speeches when serving as members of any council or committee by being un-dismissable during their years on those bodies and for one year after their term.

The partners' share in the profits, which as workers they have helped to produce and which as co-owners they have title to receive, amounts annually to 50 percent of the company's profits; after taxes and loan interest or fixed stock dividends have been paid. (Since all voting stock was retired into the employees' and their trustees' hands, stock now issued to the general

---

*Components # 3 and # 1, respectively, chapters 6 and 4, below.
† Components # 4 and # 2, discussed in chapters 7 and 5, below.

public for the purposes of raising capital is at fixed interest, 7–1/2 or 5 percent. It carries no voting rights unless dividends go three or more months into arrears, which has never happened but can serve as one motivation to keep the company profitable.) In 1963 that resulted in a bonus of 12 percent for every employee—an extra 1–1/2 months' pay. Employees receive this bonus in stock, but can convert it to cash on the open market. (Flanders, et al., 1968: 45–50, 102–106; Farrow, 1964: 89).

Under this complex system of democratization the John Lewis Company has fared exceedingly well economically, paying its partners consistently more than the retail industry's average wage (even without the annual bonus), growing yearly in sales about twice as much as other stores, and having become "the standard by which the efficiency of other retailers is judged." (*The Financial Times*, 1967, cited in Derrick 1969: 24–25; Flanders, et al., 1968: 38, 98). The working experience of its employees, as measured by the survey conducted by Flanders, Pomeranz and Woodward (1968: 130) "is, . . . judged by the usual standards of employment relationships . . . a highly satisfactory one. There was little evidence of that alienation of rank-and-file members so frequently found in modern business organizations." Of course, many partners do have dissatisfactions, which they express at committee or council meetings, in the *Gazette*, or privately. And one can conceive of greater degrees of democratization in each of the four areas—decision-making, distribution of the surplus, company knowledge, and individual rights—for the John Lewis Company. Evidence of greater democratization being gradually attained was reported for certain regions of John Lewis's membership (Flanders, 1968: 179), but there are still serious obstacles to be overcome. The most important ones seem to be the considerable concentration of power in the post of chairman, the self-selective nature of top management, and the restriction of council powers to mere advice or recommendations.

THE AMERICAN CAST IRON PIPE COMPANY*

Another attempt at employee-ownership and participation is the American Cast Iron Pipe Company of Birmingham, Alabama, a producer of valves, tubes, large-scale pipe and pipe fittings, and industrial coke (Bentley, 1925; Employees' Manual, 1969). The company was founded in 1905 by John J. Eagan and Charlotte Blair and turned over to its workers in 1922 upon Eagan's death with the intention that "service be ensured both to the purchasing public and to labor on the basis of the Golden Rule" (Codicil to Will of J. J. Eagan, quoted in Employees' Manual, 1969: 9–10). Though a smaller company than the John Lewis Partnership and supposedly guaranteeing its rank-and-file employee-owners more formal decision-making power, ACIPCO has not lived up to its claim to being a very democratic workplace.

The system of self-governance was formally established to run as

---

*This section was published in a lengthier form in the collection, *Democratizing the Workplace: from job enrichment to worker control* (Cambridge, Massachusetts: AFSC, 1973).

follows. Every year, employees elect six of their number in secret balloting as representatives to a board of operatives (workers' council), on which sit already six employee-representatives from the previous year. These twelve workers plus the five chief officers of the company (management board) comprise the trustee owners of the company stock. As trustees, the two groups of management and employee representatives annually choose the company's board of directors from representatives of management, factory, and clerical workers, and company branches (see Figure 3.2). This board also includes four outside directors, in line with Eagan's intention that the company be "operated equally in the interest of the public" (Employees' Manual, 1969: 6). This board meets monthly to review reports from each of the company's officers (whom the directors have appointed and salaried), and sets overall policy on sales, finance, production, advertising, etc., or delegates such decisions to the board of management.

Besides sitting jointly with management to select the board of directors, the workers' board of operatives advises management at any time on its own initiative. Company books are to be open to them by right at all times* and information is further circulated to all employees on a regualr basis via an internal newspaper, *ACIPCO News* (Employees' Manual, 1969: 76). Workers participate on a joint basis with managers in the works' disciplinary Council, which exercises judicial functions regarding infraction of work rules.†

Despite the democratic possibilities of ACIPCO's structure the overlap in membership between the board of directors and the board of management makes the workers' representatives quite a minority in most policy-making by the company. And the very low frequency of turn-over in directors and management positions (despite the annual elections) also limits seriously the rank-and-file's contribution to policy-making.

The effect of these structural patterns was confirmed most recently by Daniel Zwerdling, who inspected the company as part of his research for the Ford Foundation's continuing survey on work-humanization experiences in the U.S. Zwerdling concluded from his interviews with both workers and managers at ACIPCO: "the employee-elected council, representatives and committees have all become a mask . . . for one of Birmingham's last great nonunion bastions of corporate paternalism. If the system ever worked to the employees' benefit years ago, it has since become a dusty and petrified version of the real thing" (Zwerdling, 1974: 13–14).

Two components we have observed in other cases to be crucial for the success of democratization are not functioning in ACIPCO's case, full access by employees to company information and an independent judiciary for settling disputes. There is the appearance of information-sharing in ACIPCO, as there is a judicial council in which workers participate. But neither of these components actually operate above the minimum thresholds necessary for genuinely democratic functioning (see Part II): the judiciary is not *independent* of management and access to information is not *full*.

---

*See Component # 3, chapter 6, below.

†One form of component # 5, discussed in chapter 8, below.

Figure 3.2 FLOWS OF AUTHORITY AND COMMUNICATION IN ACIPCO

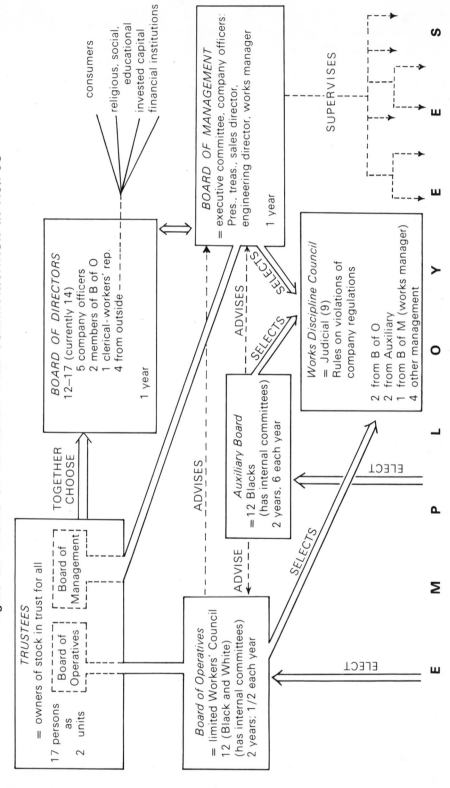

Furthermore, these related conditions have affected the consciousness of the employees (another critical component*) intimidating them to the extent that most of them refrain from making use of the remaining formal democratic possibilities.

The economic feedback component also observed to be crucial in other cases of democratization† is present at ACIPCO, however. Profits are distributed quarterly to all employees, including pensioners, at amounts up to 6 percent of their income for that quarter. Surplus earned by the company beyond that amount and not needed for taxes or capital expenditures is split 50–50 between the company treasury and all employees (Employees' Manual, 1969:41).

Economically the company has fared quite well. Over a period of 50 years it has grown from a few hundred to nearly 3000 employees and has been recognized for creating major advances in iron and steel pipe manufacture (Bentley 1925:6–7, 69). Its current sales average between $70–80 million annually (Poor's, 1969:66).

As one can see from the experiences of John Lewis and ACIPCO, worker-ownership is not enough by itself to ensure a great degree of worker power. The final case in this chapter, Scott-Bader Commonwealth, tried several different systems of self-government before its members were satisfied they had created a form which would sustain and promote internal democracy.

THE SCOTT-BADER COMMONWEALTH

The Scott-Bader chemical firm of Wollaston, Britain, operated as an individual proprietorship for twenty years, until 1951 (Farrow, 1965; Blum, 1968:ch. 7). In that year, its owners, Ernest and Godric Bader, gave 90 percent of their stock to the employees. The remaining 10 percent they reserved to themselves, attaching to it emergency takeover powers which have never been exercised. In 1963 they relinquished even the 10 percent, transferring all rights of ownership to seven trustees of which they became two, the five others being chosen by the company's employees and their elected representatives.

All members of the Commonwealth meet at least annually, and often twice a year, to decide on any proposed investment that would exceed £10,000 ($24,000), to distribute the year's profits, and to set salaries (no one is on wages anymore). In these general meetings, the commonwealth members also elect trustees, community-council members, and directors of the board (see Figure 3.3), approve or reject management's conduct of the company during the last year, and make new by-laws for the company if needed. Although employees' powers are considerable at Scott-Bader, they were achieved gradually, through experiment and re-evaluation, not all at once (Blum, 1968:ch. 5, 12, 16). Even at the outset, in 1950–1951, it was realized that self-management is so different from the conventional employment experience that incoming employees should be given six months to

---

*The subject of chapter 9, below.
†Presented as chapter 5, below.

Figure 3.3 FLOWS OF AUTHORITY AND COMMUNICATION IN THE SCOTT-BADER COMMONWEALTH

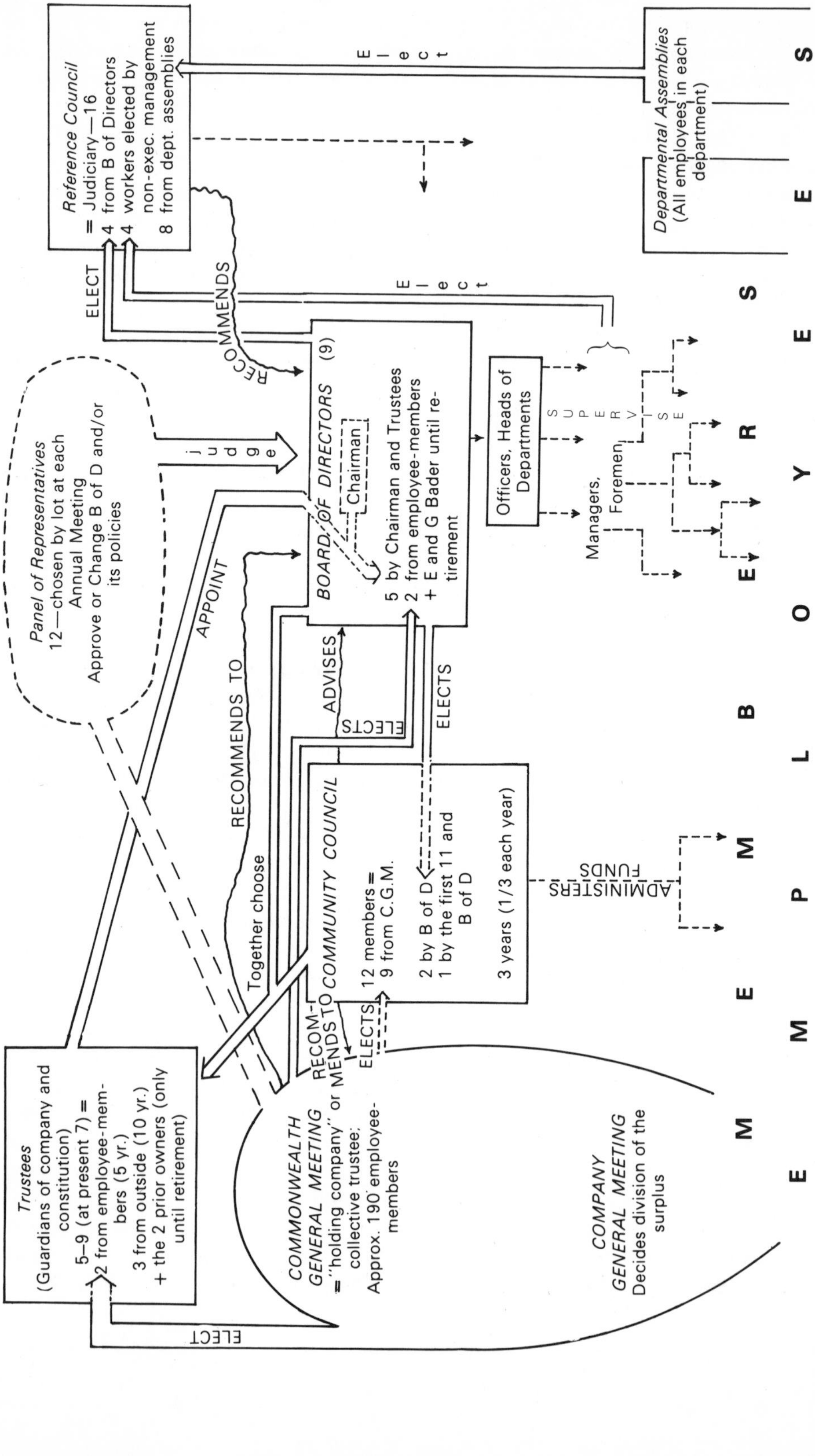

Reference Council
= Judiciary—16
4 from B of Directors
4 workers elected by
non-exec. management
8 from dept. assemblies

Departmental Assemblies
(All employees in each department)

ELECT

RECOMMENDS

Elect

Panel of Representatives
12—chosen by lot at each Annual Meeting
Approve or Change B of D and/or its policies

judge

BOARD OF DIRECTORS (9)
Chairman
5 by Chairman and Trustees
2 from employee-members
+ E and G Bader until re-tirement

Officers. Heads of Departments

Managers, Foremen

SUPERVISES

Trustees
(Guardians of company and constitution)
5–9 (at present 7) =
2 from employee-members (5 yr.)
3 from outside (10 yr.)
+ the 2 prior owners (only until retirement)

APPOINT

RECOMMENDS TO

Together choose

ADVISES

ELECTS

ELECTS

COMMUNITY COUNCIL
12 members =
9 from C.G.M.
2 by B of D
1 by the first 11 and B of D
3 years (1/3 each year)

RECOM-MENDS TO

ELECTS

ADMINISTERS FUNDS

COMMONWEALTH GENERAL MEETING
= "holding company" or collective trustee:
Approx. 190 employee-members

COMPANY GENERAL MEETING
Decides division of the surplus

ELECT

EMPLOYEES

MEMBERS

get used to their new jobs and to the atmosphere of their new company before participating with a vote in any of its decision-making meetings. As the company expanded more rapidly in the late 1950s and early 1960s, the delay in participation by incoming employees was extended to two years, so as not to swamp the still young democratic experiment with untrained members. Thus in Scott-Bader there exist two general bodies: the company — all employees, about 315 persons — and the governing Commonwealth, with about 210 members, although that number is steadily increasing.

All employees, whether Commonwealth members or not, participate in the departmental assemblies (see Figure 3.3), which may discuss any matter of interest to the employees. In the early years, the departmental assemblies were especially active in proposing ways to deepen democratization. They also formulated improvements in company productivity and served as forums for grievances. (Grievances were also handled by the Chemical Workers' Union local, which had organized the plant before the conversion to democratization.) From the departmental assemblies all employees elect representatives to an appeals board (the "Reference Council") which endeavors to ensure due process and to protect employees' individual rights.* The reference council exercises final authority to settle complaints or disputes referred to it by *any* member of the company, whether rank-and-file or management. All other company-governing bodies are participated in only by Commonwealth members.

Besides fundamental decisions taken by the whole Commonwealth at its semiannual general meetings, the company governs itself through an elected community council and a board of directors (see Figure 3.3). The board's responsibilities are to carry out the basic mandate of the general meeting, to keep the company profitable and attend to the other usual tasks of company directors, and to keep the rest of the company members informed of options possible in future decisions that the whole membership will have to make. Sharing in this task, and serving as a mid-way station between the board and the general membership, is the community council. Half of its members are representatives from the plant, one-third are from the research laboratories, one-sixth from the clerical staff and full-time managers, and one outside person from the surrounding community (Blum, 1968:96). The community council is an initiating and advisory organ to both the board and general meeting. It serves somewhat as the general meeting in miniature, providing continuous communication between representatives of management and rank-and-file on crucial issues approaching a decision. It is here that most of the changes in Scott-Bader's internal government were first formulated. The community council is entitled to consider any matter whatsoever relating to the company. This includes all issues that are the responsibility of the directors and the trustees. Thus nothing may rightfully be kept from the employees. The council also decides on entrance of new members to the Commonwealth. In general, the community council has functioned as a watchdog over management for the company's other members, reminding management of its duties and obligations in specific instances (Blum, 1968:99).

---

*Necessary component # 4, analyzed in Chapter 8 of Part II.

Full-time managers are further supervised by the total Commonwealth through a unique organizational mechanism invoked annually at the general meeting. Twelve members are selected by lot, as a kind of jury, to approve or state reservations on the board of directors' conduct of company business over the preceding year. If this panel of representatives should decide that the board's performance has not been satisfactory the board is given three months maximum to take appropriate remedial action. Then it must report back to the Commonwealth, which resumes its general meeting for this purpose. Another twelve persons are then selected by lot as representatives of the whole Commonwealth and are asked to render their judgment. If this panel approves, then business may proceed. If not, then the task falls on the trustees to decide which directors may need to be replaced.

This unique method, rather than direct election of all directors (only two of the seven are directly elected), has been found by the Commonwealth to provide the best check on management's performance. It leaves management free of the pressures of a personality contest, which direct election of leaders can too often become (e.g., in some plywood co-ops), yet keeps the management accountable to the general opinion.

Trustees of the company serve only as long-term guardians of its health. The majority of the trustees are chosen from outside the company for terms of ten years by the community council and the board of directors. They are selected for their individual interest in maintaining and furthering democratic and communitarian modes of social life. At present the outside trustees include the British Chemical Workers' Union's national President and a woman professor of sociology from the London School of Economics. These external trustees and two others elected by the rank-and-file must approve any constitutional changes decided by the commonwealth general meeting, and also must choose the five non-elected directors. The trustees can make specific policy decisions for the company only if it should begin to operate at a loss, which has not happened to date (1974).

After participation and decision-making, a crucial component observed repeatedly in cases of democratization has been availability of management-level information.* This is accomplished in Scott-Bader by circulation to all members of an internal newsheet, the *Fortnightly News*, (Blum, 1968:108) besides the exchange of information that occurs via the aforementioned representative councils and assemblies.

A third helpful component, sharing of profits,† is operationalized in Scott-Bader as follows. As a matter of principle, company income above the sum of materials costs and salaries is regarded not as profits but as common earnings, and hence the total membership must decide how it shall be spent. Rules were established to conserve at least 60 percent for consolidation and expansion of the enterprise, to distribute no more than 20 percent as bonuses, and to donate an equal sum to some outside social or community prupose (cultural and peace organizations have predominated). Over the years, Commonwealth meetings have voted themselves actually less than the allowed amount for bonuses, only 10 percent, in fact, and have returned for the company's financial strength more than the required

---

*Chapter 6, below.
†Chapter 5, below.

60 percent. The donation to social causes is made in recognition of the fact that the external society has contributed to the company's income, in particular through public services such as education and transportation. Society deserves to be recompensed, therefore, in areas which its economic system does not yet support well enough, such as culture or education (Farrow, 1965:99).

There are strong indications that the members' outlook, now that they own and co-manage the company, no longer matches the stereotype of an industrial worker who seeks continually higher wages and the-company-be-damned. The traditional fear of entrepreneurs that workers will "drink up the plant" once brought into the decision-making is not confirmed here. To the contrary, Scott-Bader workers seem able to combine the interests of the whole enterprise with their own personal interests and to determine a realistic limit where increasing their personal returns further would endanger the company's economic viability. Now also the workers, not just managers, wish the company to retain sufficient funds in order to prosper, since it is, after all, the workers' basic source of income. Also their experience of "the company" is no longer a separate set of bosses giving orders from above but more nearly a group of peers with a common future. Such a changeover from conventional to new attitudes* is here demonstrated to be possible even with a *turnover* of employees; though turnover is extremely low in this firm, old members do retire or sometimes leave, and expansion has brought in new members.

Democratized governance of the company has been accompanied by economic success. Yearly sales now total more than £2,000,000 and the company has doubled in size (from 150 to 315 employees) in the fifteen years of democratization. Indeed, it might have grown even larger had not the membership decided to take the alternative of founding a new company and commonwealth (Trylon, Ltd.) rather than see Scott-Bader become too large for effective control by the general membership (Hurst, 1971:4).

Scott-Bader's gradual and continuous transfer of power and responsibilities to employee-members did not rely on an above-average set of employees. These were persons who had worked in the traditional industrial atmosphere for years before Scott-Bader began democratization. They had learned to view industrial relations as an antagonistic struggle between selfish capital and defensive labor and gone on strike just two years before the democratization began. Managing personnel also were not all exceptional, having been taught at one time or another to fear any reduction of management prerogatives. There was also an attitude held by some employees which might have hindered any sharing of power: a reluctance to give up reliance on their "betters" and to take responsibility for decisions that would affect the economic survival of the firm. Yet gradually, and with frequent discussion, searching, evaluation, and re-examination, the employees and managers of this company learned new attitudes helpful for self-governing, and evolved a system for distributing decision-making and economic gains more equitably among all concerned.

Their experiment is still evolving, and fortunately, more experience will be available from which to draw further data.

---

*Another crucial component, examined as chapter 9, below.

Part II

MODELING THE INTERNAL DYNAMICS OF WORKPLACE DEMOCRATIZATION

Taking all the aforementioned concrete experiences of workplace democratization, whether partial or advanced, we have derived a list of six minimally necessary components.* They were selected according to the criteria explained in Chapter 1. There we stated our decision-rule that only components which the case material suggested were necessary for the maintenance of democratization would be included in this first-stage model. The criteria were: systemic and economic self-maintenance; the sub-set within that of a democratic management process, meaning managers accountable to the managed and participation available to all; and humanization, further specifying the democratic management process to be neither manipulative nor fundamentally alienating to the members. The last two criteria have the character of ideal-type specifications. In actuality, one does not find democratic and non-democratic organizations, or humanistic and non-humanistic organizations. Rather, what one finds are components that enable organizations to move towards greater democratization and towards greater humanization (or less de-humanization).

So far in our analysis, the following six components have emerged which, working together, satisfy these criteria. If any one of the six is not present then democratization decays, or a crisis occurs demanding establishment of the missing component(s). The six components are:

1. Participation in decision-making, whether direct or by elected representation. (Though this requirement seems obvious there are schemes calling themselves "economic democratization"— such as profit-sharing—which have not included participation in decision-making.)
2. Frequent feedback of economic results to all employees (in the form of money, not just information).
3. Full sharing with employees of management-level information and, to an increasing extent, management-level expertise.
4. Guaranteed individual rights (corresponding, it turns out, to the basic political liberties).
5. An independent board of appeal in case of disputes (composed of peers as far as possible).
6. A particular set of attitudes and values (a type of consciousness).

---

*For discussion of other components not demonstrated to be as minimally necessary, but still helpful, to democratization see pages 118–120.

Each of these components may develop over time, changing into a different form and operating at a different level of intensity. Thus, a more correct conceptualization of the components is as *categories* of forms, with each component-category still expressing one basic function.

Because these categories are concretely connected to each other by worker and management behavior, the level of development within each category is affected by the level of development in the others. For example, participation in decision-making might be strong at the start in a certain enterprise, while economic return and information to employees might be quite minimal. In that case, the linkages between these three factors will put pressures on the stronger to degenerate (participation, in this example), or on the weaker to strengthen (economic return and information to employees), and new forms will, therefore, emerge in each of the effected categories.

4

First Necessary Component:
Participation in Decision-Making

Minimally, democratization begins with the establishment of an upward flow of criticisms and suggestions from the managed to their managers. This rests on the recognition that each member of an organization—no matter how low on the authority scale—has his or her special area of competence and that this competence is developed daily in the employee's particular task and sphere of operations. By guaranteeing every employee a regular opportunity to contribute that knowledge to the organization's decision-making, the organization gains from democratization in at least two important respects: (1) the new feedback from employees can be an important source of innovation (Smith, 1952:5; Blumberg, 1968:Ch. 5 and 6), and (2) it can serve to monitor and correct the organization's performance (Schultz, 1958:55–56).

In a completely democratized system, the upward flow expands to include selection of managers by the managed; in such cases it equals or outweighs the downward flow of instructions and information from the managers to the managed. A *circular* pattern of authority is, therefore, said to exist in fully democratized organizations, daily managerial authority downward being balanced by employees' ultimate power to remove the managers, plus employees' frequent upward input into policy-making at almost every level.

Between full and minimal democratization lies a multitude of forms, which analysts have categorized in almost as multitudinous a fashion (Garson, 1974). In order to comprehend and systematize the relevant experience, we propose to focus initially on three dimensions of participation:

1. The *degree* of control employees enjoy over any single decision,
2. The *issues* over which that control is exercised, and
3. The organizational *level* at which it is exercised.

Each of these dimensions is manifested in practice by a wide range of forms, as illustrated in Figures 4.1, 4.3, 4.6, and 4.7. (We have not attempted in these figures to present every possible manifestation but merely to identify significant points along each dimension and to show where concrete cases belong.)

In Figure 4.1, the amount of employee influence over any given decision rises as one goes upwards in the chart. Basic forms of employee input into decision-making are described on the left half of the diagram.

Figure 4.1

DIMENSION I: DEGREE OF CONTROL
(Amount of Employees' Influence Over Any Decision)

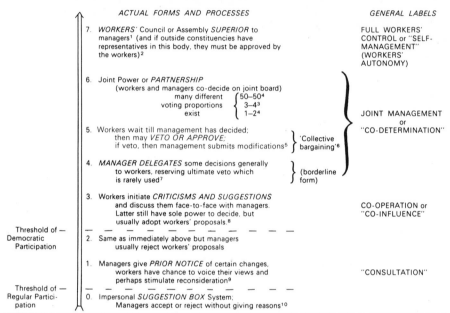

Illustrative Cases: [1]—US plywoods [2]—Czechoslovak state-owned enterprises 1968–69 [3]—Czechoslovak Mines 1921–38 [4]—West German Coal and Steel Industry 1947 [5]—Schuchman [6]—US Labor unions [7]—Heller and Rose [8]—Most Scanlon Plan firms, USA; and Safety Rules Committee in Gouldner's Gypsum Company [9]—Likert [10]—Lesieur

The labels usually assigned to such participation processes as systems are given on the right side, in quotation marks. Currently there is much controversy over just which names are most appropriate for each stage of employee influence. For this reason we have used quotation marks and have included alternate names in this column. In our judgment, this selection reflects a likely consensus.

Several important issues are involved in this dimension of employee influence. Particularly at the extreme top and bottom there are thorny questions still unresolved in the literature. At the bottom, there is the question: *Where does participation really start?* At the top, is the question of whether *full sovereignty by workers* is the most equitable way to run society's economy.

Beginning at the bottom end of the spectrum, we ask: Is a suggestion box or occasional inquiry by a manager enough to be considered employee participation? On balance, the answer seems negative for the following reasons. Systems which work via a suggestion box or other bureaucratic channel not allowing for adult, face-to-face discussion of the proposal between employee and manager tend to preserve the identification of employee as someone solely managed and ruled. Employees do not become co-manager; there is no regular weekly or monthly consultation between them (or their chosen representatives) and higher level managers who are making decisions. Employees are not even present when the decisions about their proposals are made and so have no way of knowing why it was rejected, altered, or accepted. The motivational effects of such irregular, impersonal, and individual consultation are not conducive to fostering further group self-government (Lesieur, 1958). Taken together, these reasons make it necessary to exclude such forms. They lie, apparently, below the threshold where regular participation can be a self-sustaining system, which was our first criterion. We have placed them at the bottom of the chart, showing their relation to other forms of employee influence.

A second problem occurs at what we have identified as the threshold of democratic participation. Below that line employees and managers do consult on certain decisions, but it is usually the manager who determines which issues are discussed in the first place, and ultimately the decisions are determined by the managers' preferences. Above this threshold, by contrast, many topics are initiated by the workers themselves and more of the decisions made together by workers and managers tend to go in the direction workers prefer.

Participatory systems may move back and forth across this boundary. When decisions do not go their way, the employees may feel their initiatives have been negated; when decisions do go their way, they tend to feel affirmed. Thus, a workteam that begins above the threshold may slip below it after a series of negative decisions has dampened the employees' confidence. They are likely to withdraw from participation, feeling "what's the use?" Such a withdrawal into cynicism has indeed been observed empirically (Mulder, 1973; Coates & Topham, 1968:464). The opposite situation is possible as well: a workteam operating below the threshold may rise from the consultative level to co-operation or co-influence after a series of their criticisms and suggestions have been accepted and adopted as official policy (Whyte, 1955:160–162). What occurs are long-term change processes which learning theorists would classify respectively as extinguishing and positively reinforcing feedbacks. These processes are presented diagramatically in Figure 4.2. The dynamics of this threshold demonstrate that the experience of participation can be a condition for its own continued existence. Such a pattern is sometimes referred to as cumulative causation (Dunn, 1973).

Above this threshold along Dimension I, we notice the mixing of two principles: worker *initiative* in the decision-making process (which we have implicitly been concerned with already) and guaranteed worker *autonomy* over some decisions. The mixture is an uneven one in the forms of participation that currently exist within co-determination and along its boundaries.

Finally, at the top of the dimension is the situation of complete workers' autonomy. Workers not only determine most decisions themselves (or outvote the manager on a joint board), but they determine who will be the management—workers hire their own managers. This top extreme raises crucial issues, particularly the issue of justice. Can it be rightly assumed that the greatest influence by employees is the most equitable way to run

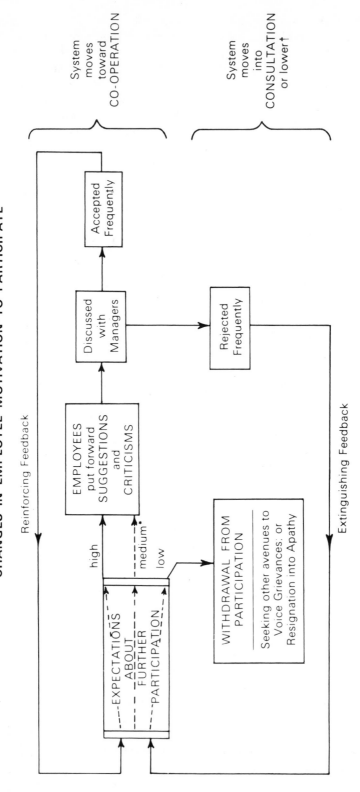

Figure 4.2

CHANGES IN EMPLOYEE MOTIVATION TO PARTICIPATE

Notes: *Tentative Trials: path by which transition can be made from low to high if the trial is affirmed.
†Or to collective bargaining, which is for the employee a withdrawal from participation in the *company* structure, and movement into the *union* structure. See Dimension III, Figure 4.7.

all enterprises of a society? Certainly there are ideologies which argue for that position. But such a situation contains the possibility of achieving merely a workers' capitalism; i.e., a system still driving for personal gain through profits, with companies unconcerned about whether their activity exploits the consumer or damages the natural environment.

One way to widen the range of possibilities at this top end of the dimension would be to confront the question of justice head-on. How can one allocate decision-control in the fairest way to all members of a firm? There are at least four value-sets (ideologies) which suggest solutions:

1. The traditional one in American business says ultimate control should go to those who contributed the capital, for they have taken the greatest risk and their contribution comprises the basic assets of the firm. Without their contribution production could not occur.

2. In contrast, many socialists say that all decision-making power should go to labor, since it is the ultimate source of production and all other company functions such as accounting, managing, sales, are merely secondary.

3. A third alternative suggests that power should be apportioned according to *relative* contributions to production, so capital would get some, labor would get some, managers and other auxiliary internal functions would get some. Also society would get some, for contributing not only sales, but also basic elements for production like electrical power, transportation, and education of personnel.

This last proposal rejects the domination by one group which both the capitalist ideology and the dictatorship of labor ideology require. But it raises other problems, for how do we determine the proportion of power each contributor to production should exercise? Even if it were to be apportioned equally, would not this system turn out to be just a bickering clash of separate interests, ultimately ineffective in running a complex enterprise day to day (Dahl, 1970:20)?

4. The fourth value-set or ideology asserts "the *human* source of all production" over the merely skill or monetary sources of production. This viewpoint argues that the human collective of the enterprise is superior to the production activities since the latter only flow out from the former (Vanek, 1972:256). Therefore, all members of the enterprise, whether blue collar, white collar, or executive, are to exercise an equal vote, to be apportioned to each person rather than to each group, on the principle of individual worth and dignity. This ideology thus rejects "all power to the workers," because it regards the fact of managers being hired under workers' control as a continuation of exploitation and as an indication that full humanization of the enterprise has not yet taken place.

But even this position has its problems. In spite of its ideal of individual human equality, a danger exists that managers will gain disproportionate advantage because, besides their vote, they have preponderant expertise. This in fact has been noticed as one of the major problems of Yugoslav self-management (Rus, 1972). Workers may often have to defer to managers' suggestions, and so may co-rule in name but not in fact. To paraphrase Orwell, some individuals become "more equal" than others.

Clearly there is no easy choice among these four positions. By rejecting capitalism one may also be rejecting considerable efficiency, which raises the cost to everyone in the community. But by rejecting labor superiority for a still more egalitarian system, one may wind up in reality with a hopeless clash of interests. Finally, if the interests can be melded, one may wind up with rule by a minority of experts: technocracy instead of democracy. We return to these questions later on.

Dimension II: Range of Issues

The second major dimension of participation is the range of issues over which employees exercise influence. Some have called this the *scope* of participation (Walker, 1974). Figure 4.3 shows this dimension ranging from the immediate work-situation of the employee up through the means functions of the organization to the major goals and goal-setting activities

Figure 4.3

DIMENSION II:
RANGE OF ISSUES OVER WHICH CONTROL MAY BE EXERCISED

to Company's Goals	
	[E.R. if this is a subsidiary]*
	16. Raising capital; economic relations to other firms, banks, governments
	[E.R. if this is a subsidiary]*
	15. Division of the profits—allocation of net earnings to reserves, investment, distribution to employees, outside stockholders, etc.
	14. Investments in new buildings
	13. Investments in new machinery
through	12. [Economic Relations with Company's Other Divisions,* if this is headquarters]
Organiza- tion's Means	11. Promotion of executives
	10. Choice of products, markets, pricing
	9. Research and development
	8. Setting salaries; management bonus plans and stock options
	7. Job security, layoffs; setting wages
	6. Fringe benefits; collective-welfare income (e.g., medical; housing)
	5. Promotions
	4. Hiring; training
From Worker's Own Work	3. Placement in particular jobs; discipline; setting work standards, pace—how the job is done
	2. Safety rules and practices
	1. Physical working conditions

Notes: *Economic Relations with company's other divisions—this factor's rank varies according to whether the establishment in question is the headquarters or a subsidiary. If it is a subsidiary, there may be conflict about whether its relations with the home office should be ranked first or third, particularly in multinational corporations (Vernon, 1971).

of the enterprise. The various issues are arranged in rank-order, but it should be stressed that this ordering is only approximate. It is an "averaging" of the values placed on these issues by American employees and managers consulted for this research. The ranking would vary for different employees, managers, industries, and times. But this ordering does show basically what workers decide on (through their union) at the bottom of the chart and what managers and the rights of capital decide on at the middle and top of the chart. It, therefore, does reflect the contemporary ordering of these issues in decision-making and suggests by implication how great a change would be involved for both management and labor by an extension of workers' influence over these issues.

This hierarchy would be misleading, however, if it were taken to indicate that influence on one issue-level automatically confers influence on all the issue-levels below it, for certainly that is not the case in real industrial relations. To take just one example, American unions do heavily influence decisions on wages and job security, but very few of them exercise equal influence over the setting of the work pace and how the actual production job is to be done. And until now these latter issues have been ranked lower in importance by most workers, as Figure 4.3 reflects (Shrade, 1974).

How does this issue dimension combine with the amount-of-influence dimension (Dimension I) in real life? Usually the combination is quite complex and not easily predictable. An interesting example is the most common form of participation in the United States, collective bargaining between unions and company managements. We saw in Figure 4.1 that collective bargaining exerts a relatively high degree of influence. That may have seemed a surprising conclusion. But now when we take into account the issue dimension, we realize how relatively few are the issues over which collective bargaining asserts that power. And we see that these issues are at the lower and middle levels of this dimension. This makes it understandable why one's intuition may have balked at the high status collective bargaining seemed to enjoy when just the first dimension was being considered. A graph which can combine both dimensions will clarify how Dimension II lowers American collective bargaining from the high score it gained on Dimension I. Figure 4.4 is such a graph. For comparison we have included the plywood companies and a hypothetical non-unionized shop. The former exhibits greater workers power, and that power is exerted over a wider range of issues than is generally true for the U.S. unions. On the other hand, workers in a non-unionized shop exert very little influence over very few issues.

The bulk of democratization experiments in the United States in recent years have been in the bottom reaches of the issue dimension. Job redesign and job enrichment are concerned primarily with issues on levels 1–4 (Figure 4.3; HEW, 1973:Ch. 4). Though some advocates of workers control are quick to dismiss these lower programs, they represent a considerable innovation. This is particularly true for the lives of workers, since those levels were until now mostly outside of their control. Unions had avoided these issues assiduously, and management therefore clung to its control over them as one of its accustomed "prerogatives." (The one important exception to the avoidance of these issues by American unions was the expansion into the production issue by some "company unions" [works councils]. But their experience was never accepted by the American union-movement leadership [Fairley, 1936; National Industrial Conference Board, 1922, 1933].)

Dimension III: Organizational Level

The third and final dimension of participation to be considered here is the organizational level over which employees exercise control. This might also be designated the *domain* of participation, in line with certain political science usages (Deutsch, 1968:Ch. 3; Garson, 1974). This is not advisable in the case of democratization, however, because many incomplete forms of democratization place worker representatives at high levels of the company (e.g., on the board of directors) yet do not allow the workers to exercise real power over all the domains below that level. An example is the French national law enabling worker representatives to join company boards of directors (Sturmthal, 1964). Clarification of such systems' true nature is made easier if we bring to bear Dimension I, for in the French case the degree of influence allowed these worker-directors is very low—in the consultative or advisory range. An illustration of the two dimensions (I and III) in concert is shown in Figure 4.5 with two other democratized cases included for comparison.

Since the different organizational levels at which democratization is actually effective have been a frequent source of confusion in discussions about industrial democracy, let us take a moment to deepen the analysis at this point.

If democratization in cases such as the French system is to be more effective, what seems to be necessary is for the lower and intermediate levels also to be democratized. Such a "filling in" of "gaps" in the organizational hierarchy can strengthen the top-level democratization by bringing more of the worker-directors' constituents into direct experience with decision-making. It also can educate them as to the real complexity of modern business, thus improving the constituents' understanding of limitations experienced by their representatives on the board of directors. Without such understanding, democratization at the top level is likely to fail, as employees turn cynical when their representatives' views seem to have little impact. This has been noticed in many Swedish firms where the law requires that two workers be elected to the board of directors (H. Bernstein, 1974). Third, "filling in" the lower and intermediate levels with democratization allows employees to exert influence at the very points where they have the most expertise. Asking them to recommend intelligently to their representatives on the board of directors, before they have gained experience and self-confidence in areas of the job closer to them, is likely to stall democratization at the start. Indeed, careful observation of the French experience so far reveals just that problem hindering their system (Sturmthal, 1964).

At first it was thought sufficient to represent this dimension by the forms presented in Figure 4.6. But that neglects what many consider a basic element of industrial democracy, namely the unions. We have already seen

Figure 4.4

COMBINING DIMENSIONS I AND II FOR ROUGH
COMPARISON OF DEMOCRATIZATION CASES
**(Scale markings correspond to the intervals identified along
Dimensions I and II in Figures 4.1 and 4.3)**

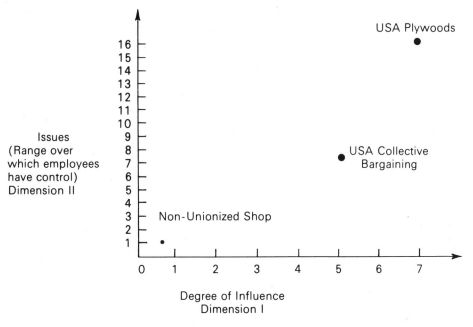

Figure 4.5

DISTINGUISHING HIGH ORGANIZATIONAL LEVEL FROM
ACTUAL AMOUNTS OF INFLUENCE

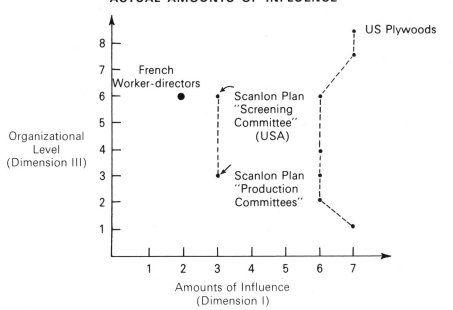

their power appear in Dimensions I and II, and generally the collective bargaining model is conceded by democratization specialists to be a genuine form of industrial democracy, though a limited one (Sturmthal, 1969; Derber, 1970). Also in Figure 4.6 we have the possible intrusion of state authorities at the level of ownership. For even in America not all places of employment are privately owned. Familiar examples are the water, electric power, and public transportation departments of major cities, and the postal service of our national government.

In this dimension, therefore, it became necessary to represent the larger number of authorities at whose levels employees may exercise influence, and this new formulation of Dimension III is presented in Figure 4.7. Here we see a complicated triad of company, state, and union organizations, all of which have levels of decision-making of concern to the individual employee. At the bottom of all three is the employee—designated by the term "self" for several reasons. The simplest reason is that with more than one role involved, as employee, citizen and union member, more of the whole person must come into play. But additionally there is the more important realization that governing, management, and individual choice-making in a democratic framework can all be forms of self-management. The Oslo Work Research Institute and the Tavistock Institute of London both follow this concept in their practical work on democratization (Emery & Thorsrud, 1969).

Figure 4.6

DIMENSION III:
ORGANIZATIONAL LEVEL OF EMPLOYEES' DECISION-MAKING POWER (Common View)

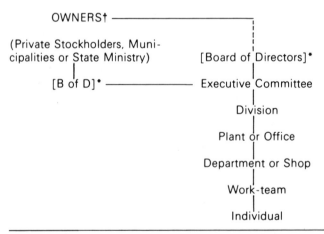

OWNERS† ───────────────────────────

(Private Stockholders, Muni-
cipalities or State Ministry)   [Board of Directors]*

        [B of D]* ─────────────── Executive Committee

                                        Division

                                    Plant or Office

                                Department or Shop

                                    Work-team

                                    Individual

Notes: *Brackets indicate alternative positions of board of directors, depending on their real power in any particular firm. If above executive committee, they do set parameters to policy; if on same level, they are to a certain degree limited by it.
†Private owners may or may not exercise power over the board of directors, depending on how dispersed are the shares.

Figure 4.7

DIMENSION III:
ORGANIZATIONAL LEVEL OF EMPLOYEE'S DECISION-
MAKING POWER (More Inclusive View)

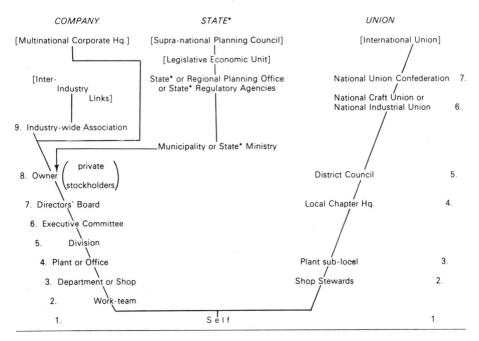

Notes: Brackets indicate alternate possibilities.

•"State" is used here in the general sense of government (whose role here is as owner or planner).

They take the view that employee autonomy begins as *task*-management and grows to *self*-management, first of the individual self as jobholder and then to larger group-selves until (we would add) the entire organization may be included within self-management. Once self-management extends beyond the individual, group identity and other attitudes become extremely important; these factors will be taken up within the sixth component of our general model.

Returning to Figure 4.7, our attention is drawn to another basic issue. One can see that the union is not equipped with parallel levels equivalent to each of the company's authorities over workers. This might impede a union's ability to lead its workers into greater influence over production. Given that American unions have largely abstained from such pursuits since the 1920s (Derber, 1970), it is not surprising that their structure mirrors this (Perrow, 1971:Ch. 4). Some observers claim that industrial democracy has already been achieved because unions exert a "countervailing power" against management (H. Clegg, 1960). But it can be seen from Figures 4.6 and 4.7 that the addition of a union does not automatically alter the intra-company power relationships for the worker.

Others have gone further to propose that unions take over ownership of companies as a way of achieving workers' control. There is empirical evidence from Israel on the complications inherent in this strategy. There, the national union confederation (level 7) is simultaneously the owner of many companies (level 8), yet reports indicate that little democratization has occurred inside these union-owned firms: i.e., employees exercise little real control over their own place of work or over broad company decisions (Fine, 1973; Tabb and Goldfarb, 1970). The reality is that the managerial bureaucracy has merely had added to it a union bureaucracy (see Figures 4.8 and 4.9) which does not necessarily increase the managers' accountability to the worker. So long as the union itself remains bureaucratized and centralized, power does not flow up from workers to the owners but mostly downward, as before. Even local leaders of the workers, within the union, are appointed by the central bureaucracy instead of being elected (Fine, 1973:233–240). In contrast to the circular flows of authority observable in advanced cases of democratization, these union-owned enterprises have a "double-downward" flow, as pictured in Figure 4.9. Utilizing the terms we have presented in this chapter for analyzing participation, the Israelis have left Dimension I underdeveloped even though they made a revolutionary consolidation across levels 7 and 8 of Dimension III. As we saw with the cases compared in Figures 4.4 and 4.5, achievement on one dimension does not automatically mean achievement on all. And consequently, full participation has not resulted. Figure 4.10 shows this by comparing the Israeli situation with other cases along the same two dimensions.

A similar situation prevails where the state has taken over ownership, East or West. In democratic countries the upward flow of power from citizen/worker/self to the cabinet minister in charge of the industry employing that worker is feeble, compared to the downward flow of bureaucratic power from governmental ministry through levels of management to the individual

Figure 4.8

BASIC AUTHORITY PATTERN IN UNION-OWNERSHIP,
(Analyzed with the aid of Dimension III)

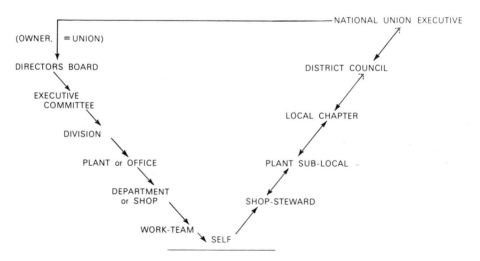

Figure 4.9

ACTUAL AUTHORITY FLOW IN ISRAELI CASE
OF UNION-OWNERSHIP
[Based on data in Tabb and Goldfarb (1970) and Fine (1973)]

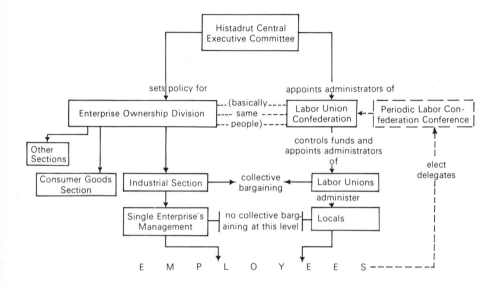

Figure 4.10

DISTINGUISHING LEVEL OF INFLUENCE FROM ACTUAL
AMOUNT OF INFLUENCE

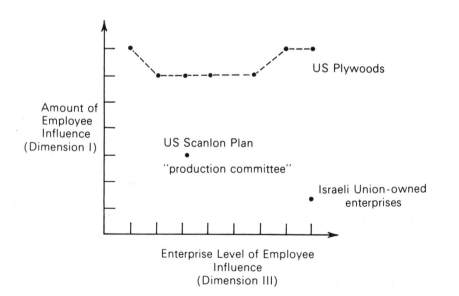

enterprise and its workers. A prime example is the situation prevailing in the British National Coal industry (Barratt-Brown, 1975). Conditions are no better in most "workers' states," because the party in power, despite its rhetoric, seldom functions as a transmitter of workers' demands to the center of power but, instead, bureaucratically controls the workers' activities from above (Mallet, 1970). [Two Communist lands, however, are major exceptions to this pattern, China (Bettelheim, 1974) and Yugoslavia (Kmetic, 1967; Denitch, 1972; Kolaja, 1965, Horvat & Raskovic, 1959)].

Change and Development

The schematic analysis presented in this section can be useful not only to cut into two different democratization systems and compare them at one point in time, but also to examine the development over time of any single company's democratization system. Earlier we discussed one mechanism of dynamic change within participation, the movement to greater and lesser degrees of influence across the "threshold of democratic participation" in Dimension I. There a feedback process between influence and motivation was involved, within the single component of participation (Figure 4.2). Many more kinds of dynamic change become understandable when we take into account all six components of democratization, as we do in Part II. First, however, we ought to complete our consideration of this one component by examining the types of development that can occur within it.

Advancement to much greater participation is illustrated by the history of Scott-Bader Commonwealth. This company began with participation mostly in departmental assemblies; that is, at low-levels (Dimension III) and on immediate issues (Dimension II) for the employees, and in mostly co-operative or co-influence situations (Dimension I). Now however, after many years of encouragement from leadership, the level of worker participation has risen to include executive committee and board of directors (level 6 and 7); the issues workers participate in cover the entire range including choice of products and market, profit allocation, and setting of executive salaries; and the degree of their influence has risen well into the middle of the co-determination (joint-management) range.

Retrogression in participation is also possible, of course, as illustrated by the fate of Algerian self-management in the early 1960s. There a lack of sufficient self-consciousness by the workers, plus the expansion of state bureaucracy into enterprise management, eventually snuffed out democratization. The state first took over decision-making power on the issues of profit allocation (Dimension II, issue 15) and purchase of resources, then on promotion of managers and annual output goals (issues 11 & 10), which the workers relinquished in trade for job-security. Then the employees found their degree of influence (Dimension I) slipping from substantial joint-management to co-influence and then just to consultation; at which point they withdrew from participation and became apathetic (I. Clegg, 1971).

More complicated forms of change occur in participation than simple development or retrogression; for example, a reduction in workers' participation is not always detrimental, is not always a retrogression. It depends on

Figure 4.11

SIMPLIFIED ILLUSTRATION OF SOME PATTERNS OF DEVELOPMENT IN THE PARTICIPATION COMPONENT

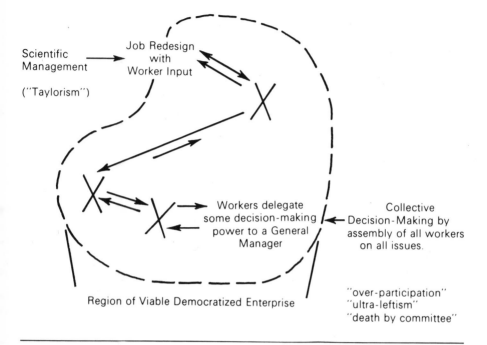

Notes: X's indicate various intermediary system-states, here left unidentified because they are best identified by the other components that come into play at these points, as will be described in subsequent chapters.

Arrows in this chart indicate possible, not inevitable, paths of development.

how, and for what purpose, the participation is reduced. As Figure 4.11 illustrates, there is only a limited region wherein democratic control can be combined with managerial authority, and the enterprise can still prosper. Some collectively-founded enterprises encountered this truth painfully when their members realized that it was better for them to delegate some decisions to full-time managers than always to have to meet and make these particular decisions themselves. The earliest worker-founded plywood companies are a case in point. The worker-owners retained ultimate authority to remove their managers, but they also freed themselves from "over-participation." Not only had that taken up too much of their time, but it was also reducing their decision-making, as a firm, below optimum (Berman, 1967:159–160).

5

Second Necessary Component:
Economic Return

Although participation in decision-making can produce dramatic results in terms of increased worker productivity and morale (Blumberg, 1968:Ch. 5; HEW, 1973:Ch. 4), it does not seem to last very long by itself nor can it continue to produce those results unless other factors are present. One crucial component uncovered during this research was an economic return to employees separate from the basic wage. By "economic return" we mean a regular monetary feedback to employees from the surplus that they themselves have produced. In various cases of democratization it has been called by different names: a "refund from receipts" (in the plywood mills), a "partner's bonus" (in the John Lewis Partnership), a "distribution from common earnings" (in the Scott-Bader Commonwealth), or a "collective-economy dividend" (NICB, 1922:67–68). This payment may be a share of the year-end profits or it may be a more frequent return from productivity margins calculated monthly or so. (A third form has been devised for partially democratized firms where surpluses from production have been barred because management anticipates an inelastic market or because union leaders fear the precedent of a speed-up. In such cases the return from higher productivity has been distributed to employees as time-off from work at regular pay [Maccoby, 1975].) Whatever its name or form, the economic return will not support participation effectively unless it is *directly related to what the workers themselves have produced.* Other equally important qualifications are:

1. That the return *must belong to the employees by right;* it will not support democratization if it is an arbitrary reward, given by someone else outside their control (e.g., a manager).
2. The return must be made *to the entire participating group,* managers included. If not, the participants may become fragmented and are likely to compete against one another for individual rewards. This, of course, would tend to destroy the cooperative interaction necessary for joint decision-making and production,
3. The return must be *separate from the basic wage.* If it is tied to the wage so that it occasionally flucuates below its current level, the workers will resent and perhaps rebel against the entire democratization system.
4. If the return comes frequently, it can usefully inform the worker/decision-makers of immediate effects of their efforts.

In that function it can help to alert them to problems (when the surplus declines), not just reward them for improvements (when it rises).

Each of these points requires some elaboration. First, that the return be the workers' by right. In practice, this can be manifested either by workers exercising direct control over decisions to distribute the surplus (as by voting on year-end profits) or by management agreeing to an automatic feedback to workers, calculated from a mutually arrived at formula, unalterable by management alone. Anything less than such a guaranteed payment leaves the decision of whether there shall be a return, when it shall be, and how large it shall be up to management. It thus becomes a mere bonus, runs the risk of being granted mostly in management's own interest, and may become manipulative, fostering paternalistic relations. All of these latter consequences can be injurious to a democratization system, for they tend to negate the attitudes of co-equality and worker self-reliance which are necessary for healthy activity in the participative decision-making component.* Dyer (1975:4), reviewing several job enrichment cases which had failed to make this guarantee, reconfirms that this principle is absolutely necessary for sustaining participative decision-making.

The second qualification was that the return be made *to the entire group*, managers included. (This also requires that in the case of automatic feedback calculated on productivity the group's output, not individual outputs, be the basis of the calculation.) This is critically important because measuring and rewarding the group stimulates the formation of group identity. Workers and managers come to see that they are dependent on one another for future bounty; it is harder then for managers to pretend to themselves that workers are expendable, replaceable, "just muscle." Workers find the joint effort fostered by these results leads to a more satisfying interaction with their supervisors than the earlier hostility. By contrast, individual rewards have the opposite effects: they split workers from each other competitively and reinforce status differences between workers and managers. Years of experience with several different versions of the Scanlon Plan have brought these facts to light (Lesieur, 1958:42), as have several companies' disappointments with individual incentive plans (Whyte, 1955).

The third stipulation is that the return be not just a flexible wage. This is necessary because the fluctuations inevitable in the economic feedback will be destructive to democratization if they challenge the security of the *basic* wage. Being a return on surplus, the feedback must vary as profits or productivity increments vary. In some periods the latter may fall to zero or even below that (when the company runs a deficit). Experience with Bat'a, Scanlon, and other partial cases has shown that employees do not want to give up their guaranteed income for the mere chance of making more money some months and risking serious losses in other months (Čekota, 1964; Lesieur, 1958). This is equally true for managers. Obviously, each has too many family obligations and other regular expenses to rely on a job which would be that insecure. Therefore, the variations must be

---

*See chapter 9 on attitudes.

confined to a range above the basic wage or salary. In periods where the company's net earnings decline to zero or become a deficit, no return is distributed.*

The final qualification concerns the frequency and scope of the economic return. This has more to do with its *informational* feedback properties than its characteristics as a monetary reward. As Bat'a discovered, this feedback can usefully inform the participants of the performance of the firm (or the group) because its flucuations come directly from the margin of surplus or deficit produced by that body. As the group's productivity or the firm's profits rise, the sum available for distribution also increases. (Of course, not all of the margin need be distributed, but the relationship must still be preserved.) Likewise, when productivity or profits decline, less can be distributed to the members which they quickly notice. This has the positive function of motivating them to seek the original cause of the decline. In this way the periodic return can intensify the firm's self-corrective capabilities, concerning the workers with boosting productivity and profits (Dubreuil, 1963; Lesieur, 1958:41; Blum, 1968) — which is seldom the case in present-day workplaces (Whyte, 1955:14–38).

But this informational function can only work if two conditions are met:

1. *Frequency:* the feedback must come fairly often;
2. *Scope:* it must come from operations no wider than those already under the workers' control.

The reason for the first consideration is that if the feedback interval is very long, it can misinform the participants, and they will be uncertain about which period was rewarding or penalizing them. Bat'a paid great attention to this, ensuring that his workers received weekly, sometimes even daily, feedback on their performance (Hindus, 1947:75–76). Several different attempts in Scanlon Plan companies yielded a rule of thumb that monthly is the longest payment interval that can still fulfill this function (Lesieur, 1958:41). The need for a short interval is, moreover, a standard tenet in learning-psychology and cybernetics (Hebb, 1949:128). And the more frequent the feedback, the more utility can be derived from its alerting and self-correcting functions.

The second condition, relating to scope, is a bit more complex but derives from similar cybernetic and psychological principles. Unless the source of the surplus (or deficit) is under the workers' control, the feedback from it will cause confusion and/or frustration (Lesieur, 1958:41). For example, in firms where workers' decisions do not extend beyond their

---

*One might ask what happens to the company's funds in such periods. Is it not a drain on the company treasury to share productivity gains and profits with members in good times but not to be covered when they decline? One system overcomes this problem by reserving one-fourth of each month's surplus to the year-end, distributing only three-fourths monthly to the members. Then, if the margin should fall below zero during any month in that year, the company draws for its own expenses on that special reserve. What still remains at year-end from this reserve can be distributed to all participants, or may be retained for the next year (Puckett, 1958:66).

shops to major company decisions such as sales and investments, it would be incorrect to tie the return to the whole company's profits. In a bad sales year, the return to the employee might be nil, although in his own workshop he put forth extra exertion and contributed to several decisions which boosted productivity. Likewise, company profits may soar in one period because of some fortunate investment or sale of assets totally unconnected to the worker's own efforts. A large distribution that year would tend to reinforce faulty as well as productive teams and so would wash out the self-corrective potential of this feedback channel. (Such contradictions are basic to profit-sharing schemes and may be identified as one of their major limitations. This helps to explain why profit sharing often does not boost productivity [Fein, 1970:9; Lesieur, 1958:41]. Profit-sharing rewards the employee, true; but he does not know what he is rewarded for. Thus profit-sharing becomes a confusing and almost random feedback, instead of a consistently reinforcing one. Employees are likely to despair of putting out extra effort, after experiencing the return to be so unpredictable. Indeed, psychologists have warned that randomized feedback leads to irrational behavior and can extinguish a previous disposition—in this case, the worker's willingness to participate—because it blurs any connection between extra effort and expected reward [Skinner, 1953].)

By the same token, where workers do have control over all decisions that affect company profits—such as sales policy, investments, and selection of raw materials—the feedback must be linked to profits. Otherwise, performance feedback will not be as great as responsibility. In such a situation, participants can develop illusions about a constancy of company profits, begin to neglect problems of the overall organization, and take refuge in their own division's productivity feedback. This would lead to fragmentation of company effort and serious dislocation (Fibich, 1967).

So far we have been elucidating the precise kind of economic return that is best for democratization. Now let us see why that economic return is not only helpful, but actually indispensable, to participation and to other major components of democratization.

It turns out that the necessity for the economic return will arise in a participatory system either as an explicit demand or as a fundamental crisis, if the return is not installed in the first place (HEW, 1973:105; Walton, 1974:158). This fact is somewhat remarkable and was one of the clues that led us to the interdependent six-component model.

If employees are brought into the decision-making process and see positive results accruing to the company from suggestions, they are likely to begin feeling that they deserve at least a part of that added value. This feeling may be heightened if they regard the time and effort they put into participation as additional labor and especially if they regard that participation as taking on some of the labor of management (who invariably receive more pay for their work). For all these reasons, participatory systems that start without an economic return usually encounter demands for the inclusion of one (Jenkins, 1973). (Of course this concern may not arise in all cultures, particularly if democratization is accompanied or preceded by a persuasive rejection of personal material accumulation. But even then, as in the case of

Maoist China, a *collective* material reward may be expected, to satisfy a perhaps parallel desire or need [Myrdal, 1970].)

The new demand for economic return becomes a crisis for the management system because either the demand must be suppressed or appeased. If suppressed, the entire program of participation may be terminated. Managers might terminate the program to prevent it from generating any more such "troublesome" demands. Or the workers might terminate it if management gives no indication that the program will be expanded. Having seen that their rights to decide are limited to helping the firm and that they are getting nothing tangible in return, workers are likely to withdraw from participation in a mood of distrust.

Another option for management would be to accede to the demands and come up with some form of economic return. This is the opportunity for democratization to develop further, by receiving its second necessary component. Management might take some detour, however, especially if it is not aware of the complex requirements in this component. Many types of economic return are conceivable, and since democratization of the workplace has been until now mostly a trial-and-error process, many ineffective types have been tried. The individual "incentive bonus" and the profit sharing plan are both insufficient for democratization, as we have pointed out, and can even be damaging. Yet each has been resorted to on occasion by well-meaning managers in hopes of creating a more democratic work environment or to boost productivity (Lesieur, 1958:41–42).

The only kind of economic return which, to our knowledge, can solve this crisis of employee demands in a way that will preserve or extend democratization is the one that meets all five requirements already explained. This kind of return gives the employees the share in the increased surplus they feel is their due, compensates them for the managerial functions they have taken on, informs them of the concrete results of their efforts, and at the same time channels to the company greater productivity. (Almost invariably productivity increases in the first stages of participatory work-schemes, practically regardless of the intent of the scheme's designer. See the vast summary of participation experiments and programs with these results in Paul Blumberg 1968:70–138). It operates as a reinforcing feedback, sustaining or increasing the employees' (and managers') willingness to participate. When combined with the other main components, a system generating strong motivation towards paticipation is in operation (see Figure 10.1).

Perhaps the most significant impact of the participatory economic feedback on the other components is that it tends to bring about a convergence between the goals of management and the goals of workers. As the Bat'a, Scanlon, and Scott-Bader cases show (Chapter 3; also Myers, 1958:87), both sides begin to operate more consciously toward the same *organizational* goal of higher output at lower cost and toward similar *personal* goals of a satisfying and self-esteemed worklife. The convergence toward organizational goals occurs because the workers are made, by the feedback component, more directly a part of the organization, benefitting economically when the organization benefits from its economic performance in the outside world and being deprived when it suffers. It becomes apparent to the worker, for example, that it is now in his interest not to be absent or to "goof-off" since that will slow down production and thus lower his total income. (In nondemocratized systems where the economic feedback component is not present, it is in the worker's interest to goof off as much as he can, for his income will not change [Whyte, 1955].) Secondly, through this component all workers are virtually brought into the foreman's function, because when they see any of their buddies slacking off needlessly they will tend to tell him or her to work better, as that affects their own income, no longer just the company's. Such mutual supervision was clearly observable in the plywood companies (Chapter 2).

The convergence of organizational goals toward personal goals occurs in part because increased worker attention to the costs of the firm begins to alter managers' sub-goals, from manipulation of their employees as a factor external to their managing group (like raw materials, loan sources, retailers, or stockholders) toward joint consultation with another part of a common operation (McGregor, 1958:94, 98). The changes in attitude underlying this convergence are given fuller treatment in the discussion of consciousness, Chapter 9.

6

Third Necessary Component:
Sharing Management-Level Information

One of the most common pitfalls in the operation of democratization schemes is an insufficient release of management-level information to employees. Workers and their representatives must be able to obtain *all* of the information necessary to make or to judge management-level decisions. Without such information, workers quickly find themselves unable to evaluate independently the issue up for decision and so are put at a serious disadvantage. In effect, the withholding of necessary information displaces workers from their position as co-managers and thus leads to the downfall of the system no matter what other efforts are made to maintain it. A clear case was the experience of Belgian works councils, where managers' reluctance to supply information destroyed workers' confidence in the system and so ended the workers' participation (Potvin, 1958). The retreat from participation reported for workers at the American Cast Iron Pipe Company* is another instance, occasioned by management's holding back crucial information from their worker colleagues on the board of trustees. Not only does participation end when information is withheld, but suspicion and mistrust between managers and the managed are generated that can reduce the economic efficiency of the firm for a long time to come. Such companies are then perhaps worse off than if they had never attempted conversion to democratization in the first place.

As we found for the previous components, the forms practised within this component-category can vary widely. Though more research is needed to establish with certainty the minimal threshold for this component, the cases we have examined so far suggest the following rule. Any degree of access for employee-participants that is less than *guaranteed access to the company books* will not sustain democratization. This is so because workers cannot be influential in decision-making if control over their information is left to someone else. Managers, owners, specialists in "staff relations" all will have their own reasons for coloring and restricting the information given to employees. And when that information is restricted so too will be the workers' decision-making power. Therefore, the crucial demarcation line between democratized and merely participatory information systems seems to be that the ruled must have a guaranteed, irrevocable right to all information they feel they need for decision-making.

This principle is actually twofold: (1) the guaranteed, irrevocable right—is fundamental, and for all occasions; (2) the information required

---

*Chapter 3, in Part I.

for decision-making—is a functional stipulation, recognizing that for each specific occasion only some information is needed. This second part also reserves to the workers themselves the choice over which information is needed in any given situation.

Without the absolute right as a first element, actualization of the second element is not possible. The disastrous impact of censorship on political democracy is an apt parallel. The designers of American political democracy knew that once information can be restricted, self-government becomes less likely and eventually impossible (Jefferson in Dunbear, 1961; Madison in Brant, 1965:Ch. 1–3). They therefore placed freedom of information *first* in the list of restrictions against managers' (government's) powers over the managed (governed) in our Bill of Rights. Empirical social science as well as traditional political thought teaches us that knowledge is power: "access to relevant information partly determines one's effective power," (French and Raven, 1959:150–167).

Beyond this crucial threshold extend various forms for facilitating the transfer of information to employee-participants and for assisting their genuine utilization of it. Frequent reports to all members on the performance of their department, on the state of the whole enterprise, and reminders on upcoming decisions play an important role, and each of these are practiced in several plywood mills. Face-to-face meetings with the managers responsible for carrying out previously-made joint decisions are a second important feature, one which occurs in Scanlon Plan firms. Frank questioning of managers by employees—not only at such meetings but also as daily encounters permit—is yet another necessary element, one found in the Scott-Bader Commonwealth, for example. An internal newspaper often arises in democratized firms, carrying information not only from company officers to workers as occurs in the house organs of conventional firms, but also from workers to each other and from workers back to central decision-making bodies. Scott-Bader's *Fortnightly News* and John Lewis's *Gazette* are two prime examples. For the latter functions to be sustained, the newspaper must be under the control of worker's representatives.

On the one hand, it may be self-evident that employees need the information managers have if they are to make or to judge management-level decisions. But the habits of managerial superiority and secrecy, ingrained over many years, seldom yield easily after a formal conversion to democratization. And in cases where democratization was not initiated with managers' genuine agreement (for example, when forced by national legislation all at once), there may remain a conscious desire to keep workers uninformed, in order to preserve the degree of managerial control enjoyed previously.

Special problems may arise even where management is quite willing to accord employees full rights to information, as in firms where management is elected or hired by the workers. In a competitive market, firms feel more secure keeping certain information to themselves, especially on matters relating to production processes, sales techniques, and future investment plans. Managment may prefer not to release this information to its employees, not out of mistrust so much as from the realistic fact that the more people who have access to particular information the greater is the likelihood that the information will get out to competitors.

One way of solving this problem, the need for "industrial secrecy," might be to transfer full information only to workers' representatives, keeping the mass of employees much less informed. This has been tried, in fact, in the co-determination system of West Germany. Although that may insure maintenance of industrial secrecy, it also has been found to reduce workers' abilities to control and advise their own representatives and thus has seriously weakened democratization in that case (Blumenthal, 1956). The Swedes therefore have proposed that managers be able only *to request* that workers' representatives withhold certain information from the rank-and-file. The final release power is left in the hands of those representatives (Bergnéhr, 1975).

A second problem is bureaucracy's customary reliance on secrecy, and the practice of hierarchies to compartmentalize information, reserving it to those who have a specific task legitimizing them to be "in the know." This has been observed in some Yugoslav firms where a third problem in information distribution has also been noted: workers ignore information on certain topics even if it is made available to them (Gorupić and Paj, 1971). They exert the natural human right to select what they will be informed about. The problem for democratization is that sometimes the range of issues workers choose to become informed about is too narrow to sustain democratic control over the enterprise. This is a problem relevant to all democratic systems, societal as well as intra-organizational (R. Dehl, 1963). And it leads us, therefore, to the second major constituent in the sharing of information.

The first constituent we have been discussing up until now is the *availability* of information. The second constituent is the members' own *ability* to handle that information. In our own society employees are still ill-trained to handle much of the economic and technical information they would need for governing their own places of work. The requisite training would have to include special courses given on the job about that particular work-place. But in the longer run, it might also require some basic changes in our general system of education, for there is evidence that this deeply affects how people approach their jobs and careers, and more subtly, how they approach authority figures at work (HEW, 1973:141–142). Valuable research on just these parameters of our nation's general education system is already being conducted by a team at the Center for Economic Studies in Palo Alto, California, and their findings may shed important light on how this might be alleviated in the United States (Behn, Carnoy, Crain, and Levin, 1976). In the case of Yugoslavia with an even less-educated popula-tion, special "workers' universities" were established when self-management was first instituted nationwide. These courses, for people still keeping to their normal work-week, include specific instruction about business economics, the national economy, and the social-political meaning of self-management (Gorupić and Paj, 1971). In our own context without a national law for democratization, it might be possible for labor unions to provide the organizational base for such training sessions.

Finally, the experience of democratization itself can develop its members' ability to deal intelligently with the complex information needed for decision-making (Pateman, 1970). Whether the workers actually acquire these abilities depends in large measure on the teaching-consciousness of their own leaders and of the firm's managers. Both sets of officials need to explain and discuss issues with the conscious aim of developing the workers' decision-making powers. That may sound like too much to expect, but it does in fact occur in most of the known advanced cases of democratization—Scott-Bader Commonwealth, many contemporary Chinese enterprises (Myrdal, 1970), and at least a few of the worker-owned plywood mills in America (Bellas, 1969). Leadership styles appropriate for democratization are discussed in Chapter 9.

Once employees do have regular knowledge of the actual state of their company, some surprising consequences may occur. It is not rare for them to moderate their demands for higher wages, because now they no longer assume the company treasury is merely a bottomless pit of riches being unfairly withheld from them (Pateman, 1970; Myers, 1958:87; NICB, 1922). The same holds true for demands for "featherbedding"—i.e., retaining useless jobs for the sake of supplying fellow employees with a secure income, as became an issue in American railroads and was considered a contributing cause of their bankruptcy. Instead, in democratized firms where employees can see that too much featherbedding or demands for too high a wage might endanger the company's survival, they can seek other ways to secure an adequate income. For it is in their own interest to keep the company going, and now it is in their power actually to change company policy. Often what happens is that the increased innovation and higher personal commitment present in democratization boost productivity and create the added margin that can cover increased wage desires or can subsidize less necessary jobs. This is clearly the case in many worker-run plywood mills. Also, ways are often found to rearrange the workload so no one is doing unnecessary work. The wage demands themselves may decline because take-home pay is already increasing with the distribution of profits or the automatic productivity payment (NICB, 1922). Furthermore, above a certain income the tangible reward of more money may be less fervently demanded if intangible rewards from self-management are being enjoyed, such as self-esteem, exercise of creativity, and group appreciation.

Thus, opening a basic information flow to employees, combined with their other rights and powers under democratization, can generate opportunities for controlling cost-push inflation, which is one of our economy's serious problems. We are not saying that democratization is a cure-all for inflation, because it will certainly not halt all wage demands; nor are wage demands the only source of inflation. But democratization does remove one of the foundations for *unreasonable* wage demands, and in that it is distinctive. And it does so not by authoritarian restrictions on wage levels, but by granting adult responsibility and the possession of a fuller knowledge of the real world.

There is one problem in information-sharing that perhaps can never be solved. That is the continually greater expertise of managers in contrast to the managed. Even if workers are trained in some business economics and do not hesitate to participate in company decision-making, some managers will always exceed them in expertise on some matters because of the inherent division of labor. Managers will be more familiar with the information needed for managing than will workers, who are in turn more familiar with their own production or office jobs. This problem of expertise has dogged all proponents of democratization, from Western social scientists (Mulder, 1971:31–38) to radical socialists (Mao, 1963). While there seems to be no way to eliminate it completely, the following thoughts are relevant to reducing the problem somewhat as an obstacle to democratization.

First, democratization does not require that workers take over all management posts themselves, replacing their managers with on-the-line workers. It only seeks worker control over managers' decisions and ultimate power to remove those managers who seem to be going against the will of the working collective. Thus, for control and for exercising accountability, exact replication of management's expertise is not required (though of course it would be useful).

Secondly, by electing a board or council that is composed of workers from the line who then specialize in management-level decision-making, the workers' group does develop a few persons who can approach the expertise of management. Clearly this is what has happened in several plywood companies. Their boards of directors, composed of elected workers, have acquired a basic (though not complete) expertise about running the company. At the same time the board members continue to work in the plant or office and so retain a worker's perspective, enabling them to represent the wishes of their fellow-workers.

A third strategy is to obtain the assistance of experts under employee control, working from employee interests and standpoint. Unions already have professional economists working for them in special research offices; indeed, some unions had very good research departments as early as the 1920s (Derber, 1970:284). These experts conceivably could extend their activity from the cost-of-living and wage-price issues now required in collective bargaining, to issues of investing, marketing, and procurement policies.* Employee councils could be assisted by such staff experts in their company decision-making and decision-evaluating, thus enjoying an independent source of expertise, separate from management's. It would be somewhat analogous to the way democracy is combined with expertise in our elected legislatures. There, too, the elected representatives of the

---

*There is, in fact, precedent in American labor history for such an expanded interest by unions. In the early 1900s John Mitchell of the United Mine Workers, in the course of bargaining with mine owners, frequently suggested the prices they should set on their ore and the policies they should adopt regarding subcontractors. He also tried to obtain for his union members reliable information on the state of their companies' markets, the true costs of production, transportation charges, competing products' prices, costs, and quality, and technical information on the character of new machinery and possible processes to be introduced. All this was with the goal of having the union co-decide with mine-owners how to run the mining industry (Derber, 1970:151).

people cannot be as expert in every field as are full-time practitioners in those fields: the economy, environment, education, the military, etc. So legislative committees hire professional staffs to inform them with that level of expertise. The competence they thus attain has been demonstrated by their ability to debate point by point with the interest-groups' own experts in the hearings process.

7

Fourth Necessary Component:
Guaranteed Individual Rights

To participate effectively in self-government, people need not only the correct information and an ability to use it, but also the assurance that they will not be penalized for their participation. Such acts as criticizing existing procedures or opposing proposed policy changes could invite reprisals from management or sometimes from fellow employees. Establishing workers councils (or some other structure for participation), or ensuring full access to information will be worthless as long as it is too risky to voice one's view because one is in the minority, or because one can be penalized by persons in higher positions of power. Zwerdling (1974) found that lack of this rights component explained the decay of democratization in the worker-owned American Cast Iron Pipe Company (see Chapter 3 of Part I).

Consequently, to be successful, democratization ultimately needs to guarantee to its participants freedom of speech, assembly, petition of grievances, secret balloting in elections, due process and the right of fair appeal in cases of discipline, immunity of workers' representatives from dismissal or transfer while in office, and a written constitution alterable only by majority or two-thirds vote of the full collective. These rights are observed to be in practice to differing degrees in Scott-Bader, the plywood mills and the John Lewis Partnership, as well as several other cases (Blum, 1968; Berman, 1967; Flanders et al., 1968; Gorupić and Paj, 1971; Lynd, 1974).

This collection of rights does parallel the Bill of Rights contained in the United States Constitution, and the rights guaranteed to citizens of most democracies. There are important reasons for this parallel which are rooted in the nature of self-government whether it be societal or intra-organizational. (Some contemporary American advocates of workplace democratization approach it predominantly from this component, arguing to workers that "it is time to take the Bill of Rights inside the factory gate" [Weir in Lynd, 1974:16].) These rights also can be understood as necessary from the point of view of the cybernetic requirements of a self-governing (self-steering) system. We shall examine the nature of this component from both theoretical standpoints.

The first right, freedom of speech (or freedom to dissent [Weir in Lynd, 1974:16],) we have already explained in terms of the need to protect participants from reprisals for voicing criticisms. Cybernetically, it is also important *for the system* that participants feel free to express their views because the confidence thus enabled keeps open a major channel of self-correction for the organization. Criticism, alternative proposals, and special information from below all can improve the system's ability to "perceive itself," which includes perceiving its own errors (Deutsch, 1963). The organization then is in a better position to seek out and reduce the sources of those errors.

Certain orders given at the top, for example, may be causing unintended consequences elsewhere in the organization because the top persons have made an inaccurate assessment of the capabilities or needs of a special subsection. Without an open feedback channel to the top which has the freedom to carry negative views, those unintended outcomes are not as likely to be discovered (Fibich, 1967). Or if discovered eventually, they still have incurred greater costs to the organization than had they been reported earlier.

Turning to positive information, upward channels kept open by freedom of speech can deliver alternatives to decision-makers for solving present or anticipated problems which the top alone might not have conceived. Previously skeptical or hesitant managers in firms that later reorganized along Scanlon Plan lines reported great value in workers' proposals (Brown, 1958:82; Lesieur, 1958:47–49). This pattern manifests the cybernetic principle of "requisite variety," by which self-steering systems need to supply themselves with several possibilities in order to cope adequately with an ever-changing environment (McEwan, 1971; Beer, 1966).

Like freedom of speech, the next two rights, freedom of assembly and the right to organize and petition for redress of one's grievances are legal stipulations to guarantee discrete steps of the cybernetic process, whereby an individual perception or proposal can be transformed into a group force and can capture the attention of persons in power and be taken seriously by them. Like free speech, these steps must be secured as rights in whose protection the participants can feel secure, or each one (assembly, organizing, and petitioning) will be regarded as too risky by most members. In that case, the steps are unlikely to be taken and the self-government process is likely to become only illusory.

The fourth necessary right, secret balloting in elections, is a familiar element of democratic procedure. It is generally intended to ensure that participants vote their actual choice rather than what they think is favored by some authority or by the majority of their fellows. From a cybernetic standpoint, the right of secret balloting maintains "channel impermeability"; that is, it prevents a scrambling and alteration of messages as they travel from the individual source (voter's mental decision) to the organization receptor and effector (official counting and declaration of the electoral outcome). If secret balloting were not guaranteed as a right in workplace democratization, our first major component—participation in decision-making—could be manipulated by a few strong-minded individuals, intimidating the others to vote their way. Under those circumstances, what is supposed to be democratization would actually veer towards oligarchy. Indeed, wherever rulers have sought to give the appearance of democracy while actually maintaining direct control themselves (e.g. in Stalinist East Europe), balloting has been arranged so that the voter knows his vote can be identified—it is not secret—and he usually feels intimidated accordingly.

Maintaining channel impermeability and accuracy is also a reason for the immunity granted to workers' elected representatives — immunity, that is, from dismissal or transfer by management during their term of service. If the representatives feared that their jobs were threatened for expressing a criticism from their constituents to management, they would be less likely to act as representatives and would be more likely to act as "selective filters," screening out the messages they thought might most jeopardize their position. This again could decrease the self-corrective capacity of the overall system, for the top decision-makers would tend to receive only what those below thought they wanted to receive. Mistakes, unintended outcomes, and the like would tend to go under-reported, especially if they were viewed by those below as being the fault of their supervisors' decisions. The system would likely accumulate more costs as a result.

In everyday political terms, the immunity of representatives is understood simply as a right of the ruled against potentially undemocratic rulers. It is a means to put the legislative body on an equal level with the executive, so the former can challenge the latter when it, or its constituencies, feel it necessary. In firms where the rule has been established with this perspective in mind, such as the John Lewis Partnership, the immunity extends even to one or two years beyond the employee's term as representative. This is so that he will not become vulnerable to threats (or to his own fears) during his last months in office (Flanders et al., 1968; Gorupić and Paj, 1971).

The rights of due process and the right to a fair appeal in cases of dispute serve as meta-rights, protecting the other rights when their application is challenged. These two not only support the channels and steps of participation as did the previously mentioned rights, but also serve as a direct limit on management's power. In particular, these two rights work to contain the arbitrary exercise of that power.

When due process and fair-appeal rights are in force, an employee has recourse to a third party if he or she feels unfairly treated by management. These rights thereby provide the base for an *auxiliary* system of decision-making in the firm, apart from the regular policy-making machinery that deals with production, sales, etc. This auxiliary system decides whether or not the participant has been justly treated by the manager in question; it can uphold or reverse his action. This process parallels in many respects the judicial function in general society, and we explore it further as a distinct component of workplace democratization in the subsequent chapter.

The rights to due process and fair appeal are unusual elements also because they can exist without the rest of democratization. Because they are concerned with a basic limitation of managerial power even before that power might be democratized through participation, they have already become widespread in American industrial relations. The grievance machinery established as a regular feature of most worker-employer relations since the 1930s is the most familiar example (Derber, 1970). In contrast, the remaining elements of the fourth component, and the other components of workplace democratization, are hardly as widespread in American business. When democratization is added, these two rights expand their area of protection and become a foundation for the other rights needed to sustain participation. Moreover, when democratization is added, the administration of these two rights is altered toward equalizing the status of managers and the managed before the firm's appeals tribunal.

Having set forth several basic elements of this fourth component— and it is possible that other rights will be added to this list—we turn to a consideration of its empirical forms, asking as we did with the earlier components if there is a minimum threshold that can be identified. Actually, researching the empirical forms of this fourth component is a particularly difficult task. Most of the cases we are familiar with were not very explicit about the rights exercised by their members. Nor did those who reported on these cases identify the rights very clearly. Generally, what receives emphasis is the package of *economic* rights accorded each member (e.g., to share in the profits, to rotate his job) [Gorupić and I. Paj, 1971; Berman, 1967:240– 248]. When political rights are mentioned, little more is described than the basic democratization structure (e.g., the right to vote, access to company books). In other words, the larger components of the model are given but not the specific elements that comprise this fourth component. In practice, of course, freedom of speech, of petition, or appeal from disciplinary decisions are observed, but it is the task of the researcher to carefully ascertain how fully each right is practiced in each individual case.

Not having had the time necessary nor the resources for such on-site inspection (considering all the cases we are concerned with), we can only sketch some generalizations from the data available to us at present. The greatest emphasis on individual rights is evident in the libertarian collectives (e.g., Spain in the 1930s or Israel's kibbutzim). This is not too surprising because the value of individual freedom holds a central place in their ideology. Cases with the least availability of rights, on the other hand, were consultative schemes such as French or Belgian works councils (Sturmthal, 1964; Potvin, 1958) where management retains its full prerogatives and merely solicits the suggestions of workers on certain issues. (See level 1 on Dimension I of the first component for the context of this type of situation.) In between these two extremes are the bulk of cases. No simple threshold was readily apparent.

Closer examination of the dynamics of the several rights suggests, however, that each right substantially requires the other. This makes designa- tion of a threshold a matter of establishing the minimal *set* of rights that can work to sustain democratization, rather than rank-ordering the separate rights. In other words, the various elements of this fourth component form an interdependent system, without any member of which the others are practically ineffective—with the exception of the two predemocratization "meta-rights" of due process and fair appeal, as explained earlier. (This is the same kind of systemic interdependence we have also noticed as the nature of the six components working together and which we will see again within the attitudes component of Chapter 9). The rights to assemble and organize presuppose the right to free speech, as does the right to seek redress of grievances. Secret balloting and the protection of representatives from dismissal or transfer are but conditions for the implementation of the parti- cipative activity that depends on the other rights just mentioned. Without the continued presence of all of them, both the will to participate and the objective possibility of participation become seriously diminished.

Similarly, each individual right seems to have the nature of an absolute: it must be guaranteed completely and for all time or its realization will very likely be ineffective. The major reason for this is given by Irving Brant, lifelong scholar on the rights prerequisite to self-government: "the power to abridge freedom is the power to destroy it" (Brant, 1965:185). Hence any modification of the right makes its continuance at even that level of strength unlikely. The case of ACIPCO and to a certain extent the case of John Lewis Partnership bear out that this is as true for rights of members toward an organizational authority as it is for citizen rights vis-à-vis government.

Guaranteeing these Rights

This brings us to the matter of guarantees. All the rights mentioned so far must not only be agreed upon by managers and managed, and be practiced, but they must also be guaranteed in writing. This is true for at least three reasons. First, any authority, even a democratically constituted one, may occasionally find it expedient to violate a basic right of the ruled (Jefferson, in Koch and Peden, 1944). This may be done with plausible justification at the time. But it tends to set a precedent of encroachment, so that the existence of the right as a bulwark in the future is less secure, and curbing that right a second time becomes much easier. Basic rights have been gradually eroded in such a manner until their exercise has become difficult and when attempted becomes labeled as "disruption" (Brant, 1965:Ch. 3).

A second reason for guaranteeing the basic rights is to protect the ruled from losing these rights due to their own apathy or ignorance. People tend to be less cognizant of the value of a particular right if a dramatic occasion for its assertion has not arisen for a long time. There is also the problem that many members of a democratized firm will not have grasped an appreciation of all the rights when the firm became democratized or when they joined an already self-managed firm (Gorupić and Paj, 1971). Consequently, when occasion arises to use such a right to prevent subversion of their democratic powers, members are more likely to lose it because of that ignorance or apathy.

Thirdly, guarantees are needed so that the existence of the rights does not become dependent on the particular individuals in power. For example, we sometimes observe several of the rights—free speech, assembly, organization—being practiced in pockets of otherwise non-democratized firms (Gouldner, 1954:221). Those freedoms exist because of the strength of particular informal relationships between some employees and their immediate supervisor. The supervisor is willing to seek their opinions and perhaps even to delegate some authority to them, allowing his employees to make certain decisions wholly on their own. Such situations have been described in the copious literature on "managerial styles," wherein such a manager is classified as employing the "participative style of management" (Likert, 1961). Likewise, Gouldner, discovering such a relationship in an otherwise bureaucratic organization, labelled it "representative bureaucracy" (Gouldner, 1954:221). When such a participative manager leaves, however, the participation opportunities usually leave with him, and the rights enjoyed by his subordinates disappear. A written guarantee helps to prevent that eventuality, because it attaches the rights to the *roles* of employee and manager, not to the particular persons occupying those roles at any single moment.

The need for guaranteeing basic rights has been recognized also by the Oslo Work Research group, who concluded that "the most important . . . need in industrial organizations is to guarantee the rule of law" (Gustavsen, 1973:21). Sometimes the state can help to guarantee the basic rights between managers and managed within enterprises. This can be via a national law that stipulates minimum conditions in the relationship, above which firms are free to arrange their internal affairs however they see fit (as in the United States' National Labor Relations Act, Derber, 1970). It can involve state courts (as in France, Sturmthal, 1964; and Czechoslovakia, Bloss, 1938) or simply the state's "good offices" as an agency upholding a right under challenge by one side or the other in a firm. Or, in state-authorized enterprises (e.g., Yugoslavia), it can go so far as a nationwide law specifying a whole series of rights and committing the state prosecutorial power against any instance of a violation of those rights (Hunnius, 1973; Gorupić and Paj, 1971).

Whether or not the state takes a role, the ultimate guarantor of basic rights within democratized companies must be the employees themselves. They must back up the written document with regular activity that uses those rights (e.g., through participation and demanding information, components 1 and 3). And they must be willing themselves to fight any challenge to those rights, if such a challenge should occur. In turn, the employees' willingness to defend the rights will depend to a large extent on their consciousness (component 6) and on their experience. Crucial elements of consciousness here are their general sensitivity to long-term consequences, their self-confidence in the role of participant, their resistance to manipulation, and how strongly they feel attached to values of equality and individual freedom (see Table 9.2).

If this consciousness is maintained, then the final right stipulated at the beginning of this discussion—that the written constitution of the firm's democratization system be amendable only by majority or two-thirds vote of the entire membership—will work to the group's benefit. If not, then there is the danger that a majority of the members could conceivably be persuaded to vote for a repeal of certain rights advantageous to them, without knowing precisely what they are voting for. But the alternative, lodging amendment power in some special elite, would be deficient from the point of view of democratization. To let a minority alter the basic law would reduce the probabilities of the system remaining open to participation by all. The problem of keeping the mass membership as the final guardian of their own powers is, of course, likely to be a continuing problem within enterprises, as it has been in national democracies throughout history (Brant, 1964).

Individual Rights vs. Collective Rights

Finally, we need to address the problem of possible conflicts between these individual rights and collective rights or needs. Though this is also a perennial problem in national politics, it is especially pertinent to workplace democratization; for many systems of democratization proceed from a collectivist ideology that, to a greater or lesser degree, sees evil in individualist systems of ethics (Lichtheim, 1970). Within the workplace, this conflict can arise as one between the individual liberty to choose the job one prefers versus the collective need for all jobs, comfortable and dirty alike, to be performed. In practice, this particular conflict is often solved by job rotation (e.g., Israeli kibbutzim, Fine, 1973) combined in some instances with a bidding system as in the plywood mills (Berman, 1967).

Moving from economic rights to the area of political rights—our main concern—the conflict would arise in the workplace as a more general challenge by the collectivity to individual freedoms such as speech. Collective need for stable administration could argue that such freedoms are simply too disruptive, that they cause delay in reaching decisions. The individualist's reply would be that to limit this right is to destroy it, for a limited freedom of speech leaves the individual participant without the opportunity to speak up when he sees fit but only when the authorities allow it (i.e., when they find it in their own interest to let him speak). This conflict has roots in the contradictory values of the democratic credo: liberté, egalité, and fraternité (Lichtheim, 1969:Ch. 1–3). Fraternite, the goal of community, cannot always be satisfied by the same policy that extends liberté, a frequently individualist goal. The problem is further complicated by the fact that even enterprises which aim at high individual freedom (within democratization) produce informal but powerful group pressures against the individual. For example, the supposedly libertarian kibbutzim in Israel admit to aiming for "a complete identification of the individual with society" (Rozner, 1965:1; Fine, 1973: 291). "Tyranny of the majority" may indeed become operative in such cases.

One solution to the conflict between individual and collectivity was offered by the Spanish anarchist collectives. Placing freedom of the individual first, they allowed for a voluntary division of the community into "individualists" and "collectivists," the former still to receive the benefits of community life while retaining their private property to the degree they could productively use it (as determined in negotiation with elected community leaders; Dolgoff, 1974). Freedom of speech and organization were held absolute, though self-restraint on the part of the individualists may have been an important operating factor not specifically mentioned in the reports available to us.

When we consider it more closely, in fact, the habit of self-restraint (and other internalized norms) forms a second possible path to a solution. As we see when considering the content of component 6 (attitudes and values—Chapter 9) a balance is advisable between individual activism on the one hand, and obedience to decisions of the whole once individual participation in decision-making has had its opportunity to be influential. A third mechanism to satisfy the conflicting rights of the group and the individual is an auxiliary system of adjudication alluded to above and examined in the following chapter.

8

Fifth Necessary Component:
Independent Judiciary

Since there will be disputes in specific instances about the application of each of the foregoing rights as well as some disciplinary disputes between managers and managed, a system for fair settling of those disputes is necessary. The participants' confidence in the justness of their system must be maintained if the system is to continue. Therefore, the settlement of rule violations must be equitable, by an authority independent of management. Just as democratization adds representative organs and substantially alters the executive process of enterprises, so too are distinct adjudicative organs discovered to be necessary in the workplace.

However, this adjudicative component seldom has differentiated itself out as fully from the legislative and executive bodies in democratized firms as has the judiciary process in our national political system (Livingston and Thompson, 1963:354–410). Also, the adjudicative component seems not to have been developed as intensively in many democratized firms as have many of the components mentioned so far—in particular, participation and economic return. Therefore, to show the full range of possibilities and to be able to anticipate future developments, our analysis first had to uncover the principles inherent in any judicial process and then match those against the experience to date in democratized firms. Three functions of judicial process seem to have primary relevance to workplace self-management:

1. To settle infractions of the rules in a just manner;
2. To uphold and be the last-resort enforcer of basic rights; and
3. To protect the by-laws (constitution) of the enterprise from violation by any member, be he manager or managed.

The first function usually takes place in two stages—an act is committed or a person is accused of committing an act that violates one of the organization's rules. This may be handled on the spot (as in the John Lewis Partnership) by a supervisor's decision that identifies the crime, decides guilt or innocence, and sets punishment or acquittal (Flanders, et al., 1968). (See Table 8.1 which presents typical "crimes" and punishments in workaday life). Or the matter may be sent to a special tribunal for decision, as in a few plywood mills (Berman, 1967). Seldom is this first stage democratized (even in democratized firms). That is, rarely is the function of determining guilt or innocence left to a jury of one's peers; nor are the distinct roles of rulemaker, accuser, judge, and sentencer always kept separate. Rather, in this first stage the supervisor often unites in one person several roles, assigning punishment for acts he himself identifies as violations of the rules.

(The firm is still democratized to the extent that management cannot autonomously make many of the rules.)

The second stage is one of appeal, and it is here that democratized firms' adjudicative processes have become most distinct from conventional firms. (See Table 8.2 and its accompanying discussion.)

The second and third functions of a judiciary after settling disputes, namely guaranteeing individual rights and upholding the constitution or basic law of the enterprise, are less explicitly acknowledged in democratized firms so far. Nevertheless they are performed, usually by the collectivity in special meetings of the whole (e.g. plywoods, Berman, 1967) or if that would be too large, by the largest representative body of the members (e.g., in the John Lewis conglomerate, Flanders, 1968). In these moments the community basis of jurisprudence is most in evidence. It represents a major principle in this component and is, perhaps, the most secure way to ensure independence of the judicial bodies from management control. When the total body of employees is the final tribunal of appeal, an employee in dispute with a manager can feel he or she has a good chance of getting a fair decision. Managers no longer can call the final shot. On the other hand, there is some danger that peer partiality might bias the decision in favor of the managed. In practice, however, this does not appear to be as serious a problem as one might imagine, because the infractions to be decided are ones that hurt the collective, not just management. The collective, from its own perspective, will not automatically side with the individual employee if the facts indicate he or she has broken one of their important rules.

Table 8.1

EXAMPLES OF WORKPLACE CRIME AND PUNISHMENT*

Crimes	Punishments
Consistently Inadequate Performance†	Demerit points or warning slips, leading
—"poor workmanship"	to (↓)
—"lack of productivity or ability"	
	Fines
Rule Infractions	
—refusing to obey superior's orders	Probation
—violation of safety rules	
—failure to notify of upcoming	
absence	Loss of Seniority
Serious Offenses	
—drunkenness	
—disorderly conduct	Suspension
—theft	
—defacing company property	Firing

*Entries in right-hand column are not intended to correlate with entries at same level in left-hand column. This varies from firm to firm.
† Rarely stipulated in advanced firms; more usually tested at time of entry.

(Sources: Berman, 1967; Derber, 1970; Gouldner, 1954)

The perceived justice of the appeals system has important consequences beyond the judicial component because it earns legitimacy for the entire democratization system in the participants' eyes. Clearly, they will cling more closely to the participation system if they know that they themselves, not autonomous managers, have the last word in how rules are applied, in upholding basic individual rights, and in guaranteeing the opportunities for participation.

Aside from these two principles of independence and commuity-base, there are several standards for administering justice that have been developed over centuries of popular resistance to autocracy (Brant, 1965:Ch. 3). Some of them are already reflected in democratized firms, others suggest how much further the judicial component might develop. In line with our understanding that dissatisfaction within partial forms can sometimes lead participants to seek more advanced forms, the full list becomes important as an indicator of possible future developments. In the first stage of dispute settlement (which has seldom been democratized so far) the relevant principles are:

1. The managed person is presumed innocent until the manager can prove guilt;
2. The proof of guilt must be by due process, involving judgment by one's peers (fellow-workers);
3. Equal application of the laws—managers are as subject to the process as are the managed.

Together these would require, in effect, a trial by jury (or some process closely akin to that) to replace the present practice of summary discipline, followed by optional appeal. One plywood company does in fact use a trial procedure in this first stage (Berman, 1967:244–245). The foreman puts his accusation in writing and the worker can protest. If he does, then both appear before an elected board of three to seven workers who decide the case. This is a regular standing committee, elected annually, which eliminates the possibility of employees packing the jury to favor a particular case. Witnesses may be brought by either side. A different form that substantially embodies these three principles is the Chinese application of criticism/self-criticism sessions among peers to settle grievances between commune members and their managers (Myrdal, 1970; Macciocchi, 1973).

In the second stage of adjudication, the appeal process, the following standards from modern jurisprudence would further extend existing practice in democratized firms:

1. Accused need not testify against himself and cannot be held guilty because of that refusal;
2. Accused may have assistance of counsel; and
3. The appeal process must be speedy and its hearings open to all employees.

However, the argument can be made that within an economic enterprise not all the standards of constitutional jurisprudence are needed or desirable. The expense of operating an entire judicial system within each company would be too great and the delay in settling disputes could be cumbersome. Certainly these problems confront the national system of justice. Exactly how much further democratized firms will develop this component is a matter we will have to wait for them to decide. Experience does indicate, however, that delays actually decline as firms democratize compared with the prevailing industrial system of grievance machinery (Myers, 1958:86).* Where the increasing application of individual rights may start increasing the delays is not yet known. As for the expense problem, it seems to be minor. The persons performing judicial functions are all regular employees and therefore receive no extra pay beyond their usual wages or salaries. It could become very costly for a firm *not* to implement these principles, on the other hand, since the system of democratization benefits from a judicial system that earns the employees' confidence. A well-functioning adjudicative process reinforces the members' motivation to participate and strengthens the community feeling that is so supportive of democratization. Finally, it may be reasonable to expect that democratized firms will continue to have fewer disciplinary disputes to adjudicate than conventional firms. This is because of the presence of the other five components, which allows resentment to be channelled directly into decision-making bodies, removes the rebellious motivation that lies behind some infractions of workrules (Whyte, 1955), reduces the ignorance that lies behind many infractions of safety rules (Gouldner, 1954:221), and increases workers' own self-supervisory behavior (page 19, above). Indeed, statistics for firms before and after democratization generally show declines in purposefully poor work, sabotage, absenteeism, wildcat strikes, and other disciplinary problems (Potvin, 1958; Blumberg, 1968:Ch. 5).

Forms of the Appeals System

Let us move now from the principles underlying adjudication to their expression in concrete forms, examining positive and negative consequences of each form in practice. Table 8.2 shows the range of forms. Four fundamental categories are distinguishable according to who has the power to make the final judicial decision:

1. *Peers* of the accused (that is, all members as a full assembly or via representatives; if representatives, they are elected or chosen by lot);
2. *Jointly*, managers' representatives and employees' representatives;
3. A *neutral, external party* (this is often the state via a labor ministry official or a special labor-settlements court as in

---

*In the grievance system, employees must take their protest of a supervisor's action first to their union representative who writes a report. This is passed up to successively higher levels of the union until eventually the company management is contacted. Their personnel office works out some arrangement with the union and if that cannot be achieved the matter may be given to a professional arbitrator. Because of the lengthiness of this bureaucratic procedure, enormous backlogs have piled up, leading not only to complaints but also to wildcat strikes over the delays (Derber, 1970:502).

Table 8.2

FORMS OF THE APPEALS SYSTEM IN WORK-DEMOCRATIZATION
(According to who makes the final decision)

FORMS	EXAMPLES
PEERS	
Total Membership	Plywood "A,"* kibbutz, some Spanish collectives
Elected Representatives	Plywood "D,"* some Spanish collectives, Czech district councils
Representatives chosen by Lot	Plywood "B"*
JOINT	
Manager representatives and Employee representatives	
(a) Direct—as one council, aggrieved present	Scott-Bader Reference Council, USA Works Councils, USA Coal Mines in early 1900s
(b) Indirect—through bureaucratic channels, aggrieved not present	USA union grievance machinery
NEUTRAL PARTY	
Professional Arbitrator	USA—many industries
State	
(a) Regular courts	France, USA
(b) Labor Bureau or Ministry	Czechoslovakia, France, NLRB in USA
MIXED INTERNAL AND EXTERNAL	
Employee and State	French "labor courts"
Employees, Managers, and Neutral Expert	Czechoslovak mines

Sources: Bloss, 1938; Sturmthal, 1964; Derber, 1970; Blum, 1968; NICB, 1919, 1922, 1933, *Berman, 1967; Dolgoff, 1974; Fine, 1973.

several European countries; or it can be a private, professional arbitrator as oftentimes in America;

4. A *mixture* of the external and internal parties (employees supported by the state, where their own participation power is so partial that this is needed; or a tripartite authority: employer, employee, with state as facilitator and tie-breaker).

In the first category, an assembly of all the members is believed by the most libertarian collectives (e.g., anarchist Spain, Israeli Kibbutzim) to be the fairest system for appeal (Dolgoff, 1974; Fine, 1973). Other firms have left this responsibility in the hands of their elected board of directors, combining judicial with legislative authority (e.g., pre-war Czechoslovak miners' councils, Bloss, 1938). And a few have tried to combine the fairness of having the common member be the judge with the practicality of leaving most members free to deal with other tasks, and so have settled on a randomly selected tribunal (as in one plywood firm, Berman, 1967:246). The advantage of peer input in all these cases is, as mentioned previously, that final decisions are most firmly accepted by the employees. They have no one else to blame; the decision was theirs alone.

One disadvantage would arise if decisions consistently disfavored a particular minority of the membership, since there is no appeal beyond the majority vote. Remedies here would have to come from an external party, such as a court upholding the rights of that minority as guaranteed in a state constitution. Alternatively, component 6 might be brought to bear, through skillful use of ideological appeals by the minority, recalling shared values to which the majority still latently adhered.

Turning our attention now to the joint system, it has the advantage of maintaining the confidence of management in the systems. This is a *sine qua non* in partial democratization systems, where management is still an autonomous element and is not fully accountable to the managed. On the other hand, this very fact may lead to employee mistrust of the system. To establish higher levels of legitimacy, therefore, it is sometimes helpful to bring in a neutral third party to participate in the company's judicial process. This we see in the fourth category, at the bottom of the chart.

One further difficulty with the joint, two-party system is that it is susceptible to rigidity on the part of each group of representatives, trying to maintain favor with their respective constituencies and fearful of being charged with disloyalty, "selling out" or "giving in" to "the other side." This problem can largely be eliminated if the attitudes in component 6 have developed beyond the stage of adversary categories into those of a mutual, cooperative endeavor.

The neutral, external-party system has the advantage of representing neither side and thus can strengthen the independence principle of the judicial system. Therefore, it is especially useful in the partial democratization cases. But since outsiders are not peers of the employees—and if they are arbitrators may be from professional or technocratic strata rather than the workers' own class—outsiders may not be accorded as much legitimacy in decisions that go against the employees' point of view. Resentments may fester after a series of such decisions and poison the atmosphere which is so sensitive and vital a factor in democratization. Under the present system, private arbitrators are already being criticized for re-interpreting agreements between labor and management in ways not intended by either party, or for compromising both sides in order to keep their favor, rather than awarding a just decision to one or the other (Derber, 1970:502).

If the external party is a representative of the state, then his legitimacy may be greater. Certainly he is backed by a greater potential power, which helps the state play a role also in guaranteeing the democratization system's integrity (function 3 of the internal judicial system). This is a complex operation. It can range from mere support of labor-management contracts as in the U.S. (Derber, 1970, including enforcement of a compact that democratizes a firm) to intervention by an activist or revolutionary state on the side of employees to advance their power vis-á-vis a manager (as in Czechoslovakia, Kovanda, 1974), or a private owner (as in Chile, Zimbalist, 1974). In between would lie court action which reinterprets existing law in ways that advance the democratic power of employees.

The mixed forms solve some of the problems that joint forms suffer in partial cases; that is, the addition of a neutral, third party can loosen up the rigidity of each conflicting party and can increase participants' confidence in the justice and impartiality of their appeals system. On the other hand, state input may not be entirely neutral, depending on the political party in power and the ideology of those appointed as judges. One attempt to get around this problem has been to leave selection of the external members to the two internal parties themselves, as did pre-war Czechoslovakia's mine councils (Bloss, 1938).

9

Sixth Necessary Component:
A Participatory/Democratic Consciousness

Throughout this discussion we have encountered the importance of attitudes for the success or failure of particular cases and mechanisms of democratization. We have seen how certain dispositions on the part of managers, or on the part of workers and their representatives, can alter the functioning of other components. Other researchers have reported the importance of a particular mentality (Das, 1964), organizational culture (Dunn, 1973), or type of consciousness (Freire, 1974) to the development and success of democratization. The negative case is also indicative: in the absence of certain outlooks and mental abilities, a system established to be democratic will not function democratically (Tabb, 1970).

This component is the most difficult to specify, not only because the symbolic realm with which it deals is less tangible, but also because a clash of ideologies occurs here (Greenberg, 1975). Among the chief ideological positions that assert different possible forms of consciousness for humanizing and democratizing the workplace are the following:

1. Managerial effectiveness,
2. Productivity and worker-incentives,
3. Human relations, stressing informal relationships and cooperation,
4. Formal democracy in institutions,
5. Workers' control, and
6. Humanization and self-realization of the working community (the worker as an end not merely a means of the organization).

To take just a few examples, the productivity/incentives ideology emphasizes economic and material values and worker identification with company-defined goals. On the other hand, the ideology connected with formal democracy tends to stress voting and the ideals of good citizenship as guides to behavior within the organization. It requires managers to be responsive to their citizenry, i.e., the employees.

In this way each ideology defines roles and expectations for the participants and, therefore, implies (even when it does not openly state) what would be the most appropriate consciousness in each case. With ideologies that require the lesser levels of participation (1, 2, or 3), the manager is required to take into account the needs of the employees for a congenial and perhaps somewhat self-expressive work environment. With ideologies at the other extreme (5 and 6), management is beholden to the workers; or the very roles of management and worker undergo such dynamic change that the organizational structure (not just a few roles) is periodically transformed. A dramatic example here is the cultural revolution in Chinese institutions (Macciocchi, 1972).

Given this wide range of possibilities, can one set of attitudes and propensities best suited for democratization be specified? In seeking an answer to that question, it must be remembered that no concrete case of democratization, whether minimal or advanced, in fact displays a uniform set of attitudes and propensities within its population of participants. Rather, the dynamic and shifting reality of consciousness in each organization is more accurately represented as a distribution of attitudes and propensities among the membership and its leaders. Furthermore, within each member, each single element of consciousness (an attitude, belief, or value) may be present to a different degree. The sum total is a complex, variegated, and changing combination of distributions that can only be approximated, even with the best attitude-measuring instruments. This is shown in Figure 9.1.

In examining this complex phenomenon of participatory/democratic

Figure 9.1

CONSCIOUSNESS AS A COMPLEX DISTRIBUTION OF ELEMENTS WITHIN AND AMONG THE PARTICIPANTS

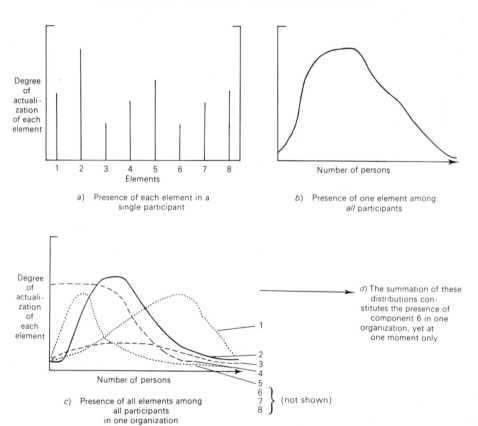

a) Presence of each element in a
    single participant

b) Presence of one element among
    all participants

c) Presence of all elements among
    all participants
    in one organization

d) The summation of these
    distributions con-
    stitutes the presence of
    component 6 in one
    organization, yet at
    one moment only.

consciousness, we start at the micro-level within the mind of the individual participant and then work our way out to the group process and organizational atmosphere that results. The set of attitudes, beliefs, and values that provide our focus may best be understood as ideal-types, never completely achieved but approached and practiced more comprehensively in the more advanced firms.

Several researchers have identified individual elements of consciousness that seem critical to the process of group self-management (Argyis, 1954; Freire, 1974; Maslow, 1964; Theobald, 1970; Bernstein and Young, 1973). These findings are listed in Table 9.1. Although the terminology differs from one author to the next, and from one discipline to the next, the habits of mind described for democratization are in many instances quite similar. They are not exactly parallel in all traits, of course.*

According to these researchers, for self-management a person must lean generally in the direction of self-reliance, flexibility, and activism. He or she needs to be able to admit his or her own mistakes, be receptive to new and unfamiliar experiences, and be able to fashion compromises with others. The capacity for self-management also includes a readiness to look for past trends and future consequences, a sensitivity to the difference between means and ends, and a strong sense of attachment to one's fellows.

Of course, these traits are not expected to be present in their absolute form; rather they indicate directions or tendencies towards which people actively self-governing their organizations have been observed to develop. Being directions, each one of the traits has an opposite direction or characteristic; for example, self-reliance lies at one end of a spectrum the opposite pole of which may be conceived as dependence (Argyris, 1954) or servility (Cole in Pateman, 1970:45). Each member of the organization is characterized as occupying some point between the two poles, rather than being simplistically categorized as either self-reliant or servile (see Figure 9.2). The same may be said for each of the other traits frequently identified as beneficial to, or, in the negative case, deleterious to democratization.

An interesting discovery was that each of the traits identified as generally supporting democratization exhibited two opposites, not just one. As they were examined together, it became apparent that one set of opposites related to the inputs of the managing process, while the second set related to its outputs. Specifically, one sub-system of the participatory democratic consciousness is a resistance to being manipulated, while the second set comprises an ability to create and organize policies (see Table 9.2). The opposite of each of these subsystems defines passive and compliant

---

*Although drawing on data from other institutions could be a very risky procedure in the case of certain components of our model (e.g., component 2, economic feedback), it is not so inappropriate in the case of consciousness. The nature of this component is such that it partakes of the general experience of the members, not just their specific experience at work (Anderson, 1971:Ch. 2, 3, 5). Secondly, the habits of mind utilized in making self-governing decisions do not have to vary as greatly as the tasks being self-governed may vary. Given the early stage of research in this area, it seemed worthwhile to draw upon self-managing experience in non-work organizations as well as work organizations.

Table 9.1

MENTAL TRAITS BELIEVED TO BE REQUIRED FOR MAINTAINING (AND CREATING) DEMOCRATIZATION

Researcher: →	FREIRE	THEOBALD AND MASLOW	BERNSTEIN AND YOUNG	ARGYRIS
His general term for It →	"critical consciousness" and "transitive con-sciousness"	"democratic character structure of self-actualizing persons"	"democratic mentality"	"Mature adult tendencies" (as opposed to child's needs)
Empirical referent →	Initially contrasts rural illiterates of Chile and Brazil with free citizens of North Atlantic: More recently: contrasts those peasants' initial mentality with their self-management after a liberative literacy education	Casework experience in European and American psychology	Czechoslovak activism, 1960s period in particular	Casework in individual psychology and in modern work organizations
TRAITS → 1.	Refuses to transfer responsibility	High self-esteem and confidence	Self-reliance	Develops towards independence. as a first stage (see #5 below)
2.	(a) Tests own findings (b) Attempts to avoid distortions or preconceived notions when analyzing problems (c) Open to revising own ideas	(b) Sharpened perception of reality; recognizes inevitable limits (d) Differentiates well between means and ends	(a) Critical thinking: (b) Seeks to separate illusions from reality (c) Self-critical (d) Distinguishes positive from negative	

3. (a) Seeks exchange of experiences	(a) Can resolve apparent dichotomies by recognizing synergistic relations in them	(a) Synthetical thinking: borrows from many different experiences;
(b) Receptive to the new (but not for novelty's sake)		(b) Ability to compromise
(c) Explains by causal principles, rather than magical ones; interprets problems in depth		(c) Expects multiple causation
4. Selects from the past; won't reject something just because it is old	Long time-sense —attention to and use of traditions —realizes each present solution can bring a future problem	Longer time perspective
5. Sense of community solidarity	Awareness of group's needs	Develops towards interdependence as a second stage
6. Highly permeable, flexible mentality	Permeated by a whimsy, openness, and flexibility	Capable of flexible behavior
7. Practices dialogue rather than polemics		
8. Rejects passive positions	Active organizer	Initiates action towards others as often or more often than others do towards him or her
	Generally feels free to say and act the way he or she feels	
Interrogative, restless		Inquisitive

Figure 9.2

EACH TRAIT AS ONE LOCATION ON A BI-DIRECTIONAL CONTINUUM

Dependent,   Self-reliant
servile

members, whose tendencies leave them more prone to being manipulated by the outputs of the managing process (column I in the table) and less able to create and organize inputs to the managing process (column IV).

A caveat: this representation is by no means intended to define fully or with great certainty the content of participatory/democratic consciousness. That alone would be the task of a book-length study, and there was no time for that in the present research. Secondly, empirical research in this area is still relatively sparse. Several of the terms utilized in Table 9.2 are still quite broad and contain a great number of possibilities that need to be made explicit by further research. All that is intended here is to present some major probable components of the consciousness seemingly required to sustain democratization. It is merely a grounding for future research.

We may note, however, that even at this early stage there are reasons for assigning some confidence to the traits so far identified. One is the substantial agreement between findings by independent researchers who drew on different cases, cultures, and disciplines. Now we may also note that each of the composites exhibits an interdependence among its traits suggesting the existence of underlying psychological linkages. In other words, the traits exhibit empirical interconnections which tie them into a mental system or character structure (Theobald, 1970). To give an example, in the central column self-reliance provides one important emotional foundation for inquisitive, critical thinking (5) which itself helps to equip activist behavior (8). Likewise in the far right-hand column, the elements of superficial thinking (6) can predispose a person to a dependent stance vis-à-vis authority (2) as well as to rigidity of outlook (1), which in turn can incline him or her to neglect unexpected opportunities (7) for action (8).

We will remark further on the interrelation of these elements below. For now we turn to some additional traits that are required for leadership in democratized firms.

Traits Required for Leadership

Special additional traits are required for leadership personnel in democratized firms and are detailed in Table 9.3. First, an explanation of why extra traits are needed. Whether he is a manager over the workers, or one of the workers' elected representatives and so a potential leader of employees, such a person comprises a special category in democratized firms—simply because he wields more power. How the power-holder makes use of this opportunity is significantly influenced by his own sense of values, by his personal goals and beliefs—in short, by his consciousness.

Researchers from liberal-democratic, radical socialist, and anarchist-humanitarian traditions all agree that for the success of democratization

Table 9.2

MAJOR SUBSYSTEMS OF TRAITS

	Relating to Outputs of the Managing Process	Relating to Inputs of the Managing Process		
		"Participatory-Democratic Consciousness"		
	I. More Prone to Being Manipulated	II. Less Prone to Being Manipulated	III. More Able to Create & Organize Policy	IV. Less Able to Create & Organize Policy
1.	Rigidity of thought	Receptivity to the new, flexibility		Overseriousness, dogmatism
2.	Servility, timidity	Self-reliance, refusal to transfer responsibility		Dependence
3.		Facility for compromise and receptivity to needs of others		Sectarian
4.	Indifferent, unquestioning	Inquisitive, interrogative		
5.	Extreme loyalty, deference, credulity	*Critical thinking:* —attempts to avoid distortions and preconceptions —self-critical —carefully differentiates between means and ends —acknowledges inevitable limits		Defensive
6.	Simplistic thinking: black-and-white outlook	Expects multiple causation Seeks to analyze in depth		Superficial thinking
7.	Short time-sense	Long time-sense		Short time-sense
Rough Summation (8)	Compliance	Resistance	Activism	Passivity, abstention

Sources: Freire, 1974; Theobald, 1970; Maslow, 1954; Argyris, 1954; Bernstein and Young, 1973.

Table 9.3

ADDITIONAL TRAITS REQUIRED OF POWER-HOLDERS

Discourages or Prevents Democratization		*Fosters or Facilitates Democratization*
1. Desire to maintain exclusive prerogatives	←─┴──┴──┴─→	Egalitarian values
2. Paternalism	←─┴──┴──┴─→	Reciprocity
3. Belief that leader must set example by appearing infallible (tries to hide all mistakes)	←─┴──┴──┴─→	Awareness of own fallibility; Admits errors to managed
4. Governing from position of formal power	←─┴──┴──┴─→	Governing by merit, explanation, and consent of governed
5. Mistrustful, feels all others need 'close watching'— hence: intense supervisions, limits freedom of subordinates	←─┴──┴──┴─→	Confidence in others—hence: willingness to listen and to delegate responsibility
6. Proclivity to secrecy, holding back information	←─┴──┴──┴─→	Policy of educating the managed; open access to information

Sources: Blumberg, 1968:23, 103; Derber, 1970:469; Mulder, 1972:224; Pateman, 1970; Norton, 1974; Tabb and Goldfarb, 1970; and Mao, 1966.

the most important attribute of this power-holder is that he have the consciousness of an educator, not just a manager (Mao, 1963; Mulder, 1973; Adizes, 1971). He must want and be able to teach his subordinates how to use power, not just use power himself to rule over them. In our terms, he must be a democratizer, not just a decision-maker.

The difference can be elucidated as two different kinds of rule. In one kind of rule, it is sufficient to satisfy the ruled by actions initiated above, so long as those actions meet what the ruled feel are their most pressing needs. This can be done from a paternalistic stance and may condition the ruled to a dependent relationship vis-à-vis their rulers. The democratizing kind of rule, on the other hand, seeks to educate the managed out of their extreme dependence on managers, giving them repeated opportunities to develop skills of self-government. It aims to have the managed take an increasingly larger share in decision-making and to have them increasingly hold official decision-makers accountable to them.

There is a crucial reason for this kind of rule being necessary in democratization, beyond the simple aim of achieving participation by the widest number. Power corrupts, said Lord Acton, in his famous epithet crystallizing an historic truth. Merely exercising power can transform a person's consciousness, displacing goals of service by goals of personal advantage, and altering his or her values and skills accordingly. The power granted becomes used less and less to accomplish the organizational tasks for which it was originally granted and more and more is used to prolong its own reign (and to reduce the power of others as a means to achieve that). Leaders of the most democratic and participatory movements have succumbed to this process, as is notoriously known (Michels, 1958).

Therefore, if democratization is to succeed, it must have mechanisms that prevent or block this tendency in its leaders. Some of the mechanisms for doing this have already been mentioned in each of the earlier components.* But a specific mentality that limits persons once they become power-holders is also a crucial component. This mentality needs to consist in the very least of an internalized norm, which carries an inevitable sense of obligation not to become a tyrant, even a benevolent one. (This sense of obligation will be more effective if it is felt as a community-wide norm, not just a personal goal of the power-holder [Almond and Verba, 1965:469].) But the power-holder's mentality must go beyond this negative injunction and extend to a positive application of his power in ways that can increase the power-potential of the ruled.

Were it just a general outlook, such a commitment would be perhaps almost impossible to actualize. But there are specific attributes comprising this mentality that can guide the power-holder in daily decision-making. These are listed in Table 9.3. On almost every occasion, the power-holder's choice of *means* will lead the organization either towards more humanizing and democratizing conditions or towards more de-humanizing and autocratizing conditions (Fibich, 1967). For example, if the power-holder operationalizes the value of reciprocity (2 in Table 9.3) and listens and takes into account how the managed feel about various alternatives in an upcoming decision, the organization will be more likely to move toward democratization. This would be true even where the workers' formal structures of power were relatively minimal. (Hence the findings on certain "open and reciprocal management styles" [Likert, 1961]). To take another value (1 in Table 9.3), if in making decisions the power-holder feels it necessary to preserve his personal or managerial prerogatives and considers it too risky or even foolish to depart from them in favor of a more egalitarian status vis-à-vis the employees, the organization will intensify its hierarchical, bureaucratic and, in some sense, autocratic tendencies (Tabb & Goldfarb, 1970).

A third important value is the preference for persuasion by open explanation (4), meaning that the ruler accepts the right of the managed to question and demand explanation for a policy and that he or she feels it incumbent to gain their voluntary consent. In contrast is the policy of persuasion by threat of force, whereby the ruler utilizes the powers of office to

---

*In component #1: balancing the managers' power with representatives of the managed, who are in turn removable from office by will of the electorate. In component #2: sharing control over the surplus. In component #3: inability to keep much company business secret. In component #4: the several guaranteed rights which enable the managed to organize alternatives to managers' or leaders' proposals. In component #5: an independent adjudicative process as refuge of appeal for the managed in dispute with a power-holder.

threaten sanctions against anyone who would question his or her policies or not obey automatically (Blumberg, 1968). These particular leadership alternatives have been generalized by Scottish management expert Tom Burns as "sapiential authority" and "structural authority," respectively (Theobald, 1970).

Confidence in others (5) is another necessary element for a democratizing power-holder; just as its opposite—skepticism about the abilities of others—underlies many autocratic or close-supervisory styles.

It can be seen that many of the propensities and values which encourage leaders toward further democratization of their relations with employees interact in a systemic way (right-hand column), as do the values and predispositions toward managerial exclusivity and privileged power (left-hand column). This is why it may be more effective for the whole consciousness to be assumed by those attempting to be democratic managers, rather than trying to take on just one or two traits as some "sure-fire" policy (McGregor, 1958). Obviously where only part of the democratic consciousness is being applied by a leader, its individual elements can come into conflict with the traditional values of managerial privilege held simultaneously by that leader. This suggests why, when well-intentioned managers have given attention to just one or two of these elements in the past, the intended results did not always occur. Such experiences often led these managers to the conclusion, perhaps prematurely, that democracy in management cannot work (Hackman, 1975).

Quality of Relations and Atmosphere in a Firm

When both the managed and the power-holders possess and exercise the mental tendencies so far specified, a certain "quality of relations" has been reported to emerge (Fibich, 1967). Informal relations between managers and managed become more important (Mulder, 1973) because administration no longer entirely proceeds from the pure power of one's position. Obedience is achieved more by internalization of norms than by threat of negative sanctions (Fibich, 1967). The manager's willingness to explain his decisions and employee participation in at least part of the decision-making reduces the status differential between the two parties. Taken together, these changes produce an atmosphere that is most often described as "more cooperative" (McGregor, 1958:89; Pateman, 1970; Argyris, 1954; Norcross, 1974).

Because the term "cooperation" can be easily misunderstood, we wish to qualify its use here immediately. A cooperative atmosphere in a firm does not necessarily mean that all conflict has been done away with. Rather, what seems to be the case is a lessening of the harsh polarization into two mistrusting camps, labor and bosses, that is so often found. There is not the extreme opposition of workers' and managers' goals that can be bridged only by a money-bargain, whereby the worker surrenders his time and his hopes for meaningful work for the money payment, and the manager has to spend a lot of his energy figuring out ways to motivate the employee to work beyond that begrudging minimum (Steers and Porter, 1975:92).

Conflicts in democratized firms will arise between participants, most

Figure 9.3

FEEDBACKS BETWEEN PARTICIPANTS' BEHAVIOR, RELATIONS, AND CONSCIOUSNESS

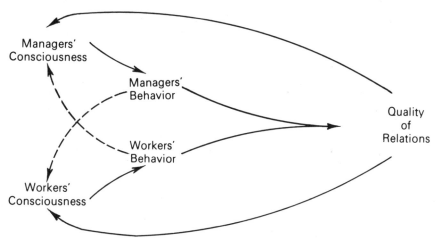

certainly. But the greater access to decision-making councils and other rights that these employees enjoy allows for handling their demands sooner and more cooperatively than is the case in many non-democratized firms. Likewise, the stereotypes held by many conventional managers of the untrustworthy or irresponsible worker have a chance to become modified in democratized firms. Through face-to-face contact in co-decision-making situations, as well as through successful delegation of responsibility to employees, a manager is brought to alter his attitudes about the capabilities of his workers (McGregor, 1958:80). This can change the way he or she behaves towards them, which in turn, and over the long-run, can stimulate changes in the workers' behavior. This then feeds back to the general quality of relations. Figure 9.3 summarizes this feedback situation.

By the same token, when the managed and the power-holders in a formally democratized firm do not both possess the set of attitudes, beliefs, and values so far specified, resentment, cynicism, and other forms of hostility characterize the resulting atmosphere (Walker, 1967:67). The willingness of the power-holders to see democratization work must be at least as great as the desire by the managed to have such rights and to exercise them; otherwise, serious frictions will tend to arise (Obradović, 1970).

Complications and Contradictions within the Consciousness

There is a tension between two basic traits: self-reliance and receptivity to others' needs. Both traits are definitely necessary for successful management of a democratic enterprise. Without receptivity to others' needs, common agreements would be hard to achieve. But without self-reliance, initiative from below would be unlikely to arise for governing shop-floor tasks and holding the management accountable to those below. Despite the necessity for both, the two traits are not easy to combine in one personality. Self-reliance can lead the individual away from receptivity to others' needs, whereas too encompassing an attachment to others can prevent the development of personal self-reliance.

In spite of this problem, there are ways the tension may be resolved in the individual. One hypothesis holds that the conflict between self-reliance and receptivity to others exists only at one level, only at an early stage of personality development. Once an individual develops beyond that stage, his or her self-reliance is no longer of a defensive kind and will not need to exclude others in order to exercise itself. Rather, the opposite becomes true: because of greater individual, internal strength and self-confidence, they are more open to the world around them, including the needs of others (Theobald, 1970; Maslow, 1954). Such persons can more calmly find a way to weld the two sets of interests. That type of personality is especially advantageous to democratization as a power-holder, because he or she is able to synthesize necessary compromises from the variety of opinions held by participants, instead of imposing one authoritarian position.

If this thesis of individual development is true (propounded mostly by Maslow and his followers), then the resolution of opposing traits that seems necessary for democratic consciousness can be attained in many people. If it is not true (or if it is true in theory but a practical way cannot be found to bring it about in large numbers of people), then democratization will have to depend on the rare, spontaneous occurrence of such individuals, and its spread beyond existing cases will be much less likely.

A different tension may arise: between the trait of activism, on the one hand, and the organizational need for stability and obedience to decisions once made on the other. Some authors have approached this tension by arguing that the organization's need for stability is always paramount to the democratizer's ideal of active participation (Almond and Verba, 1963).

Others take the view that the activism/obedience problem is part of an inevitable dialectic between authority and participation. Leaders such as Mao have sought to make use of this dialectic by periodically encouraging activism among the populace ("the masses") and alternatively calling for consolidation of new authority structures (into a "proletarian dictatorship"). They thus seek to resolve the problem by alternating cycles.

A different conceptualization for resolving this tension by cycles emerges from the cases described in Chapters 2 and 3. There we saw circular flows of authority: up from participants when they are choosing their managers and setting annual policy directly; downward when the elected directors make decisions that are obeyed by the rest of the workers. This circular pattern demonstrates that the alternation between obedience and activism can occur within a stable authority structure. It need not always take the form of a dialectical revolution.

A third central conflict in the consciousness of democratized enter-prises is the clash of values between maximizing economic goals on the one hand and maximizing democratic and humanistic goals on the other. Sometimes this problem might appear to resolve itself, because a significant increase in productivity can result from the release of human forces under democratization. But there will be times in a democratic enterprise when efficiency calls for bypassing the democratic route, or when economic profitability calls for a de-humanizing pace of work.

What can be done in such cases? One answer that has been suggested is for enterprises to make the prior commitment that in such conflicts, the humanization goal will take priority (Dunn, 1973). Maximal profitability of the enterprise may then suffer, but basic economic viability of the firm will not be sacrificed. Under such a policy the economic realities of production, market competition, and so forth, remain, but only as constraints on choices of management, no longer as their central governing priorities. In a sense this would merely reverse the policy of conventional firms, which puts the goal of maximum economic performance first and allows it occasionally to be constrained by certain human considerations (safety, fatigue, etc.).

The Question of Thresholds

Determining the minimal threshold within this component is vastly more difficult than for the other components. Much more research experience must still be gathered before the threshold (or thresholds) can be specified. But the research conducted so far generates some light.

The question of "how much?" really involves three issues:

1. How developed must the consciousness be *in any individual* before he or she can participate contributively in a democratized firm?
2. How developed must the consciousness be *in any firm* before it serves as a secure foundation for democratization?
3. *How many* of the individual elements are needed before the consciousness can be said, by definition, to exist?

We can offer answers to each of these questions not in detail, trait after trait, but by presenting some general considerations which indicate the outline of likely, long-term answers.

Considering the first issue, it seems that a person need not have all the central columns' traits (Table 9.2) merely to begin participating in democratization. Certainly, different roles within the self-governing process will require different degrees of the participatory consciousness. And the more a person wishes to exercise a leadership role in particular, the more active, initiatory, skillful in organizing, and resistant to manipulation he or she will have to be.

The second question finds its initial answer in the following requirement: there must be enough activity by the managed to keep the managers *accountable* to the former. In other words, enough elements of this consciousness must reside among the managed to activate them periodically so that management remains bound by their general views and interests. Of course, democratic orientations must reside among the managers also or the firm will not run smoothly. But in the long run, democratization is unlikely to survive if only the managers understand democracy. They must be held to democratic practice by the managed.

This logically leads us to the third issue concerning the minimal set of traits that qualifies as a participatory/democratic consciousness. If the answer being demanded is purely conceptual or definitional, then the most that can now be offered are the composites displayed in Tables 9.2 and 9.3. But if the answer may be phrased in terms of practice, a bit more can be said. The two prior considerations can indicate that, in practice, individuals lacking some of the listed traits may interact with others in the same firm who lack other necessary traits but possess some of the first traits, and the firm will still experience occasional participatory decision-making. A well-known example in the organizational literature is Alvin Gouldner's description of a gypsum company's safety committee (which he called a "representative bureaucracy"). According to Gouldner's description, the supervisor had the traits of reciprocity and preference for persuasion, but not full acceptance of rule by merit (he would not actually let the workers set the safety policy). The workers approached the safety question with self-confidence in their own knowledge on that issue, although they did not generalize that self-confidence to other issues nor exhibit a long time-sense (Gouldner, 1954:221). As this example also shows, the application of partially participatory consciousness is likely to remain confined to one issue and to the immediate area of the firm where it takes place. It does not easily spread to other parts of the company, nor to other issues. So this degree of consciousness seems to lie below the minimum threshold.

Two more clues for ascertaining the minimal composition of participatory/democratic consciousness come from the following considerations. One is the *inherent interrelatedness* of several of the identified elements, each one reinforcing or facilitating the development of another, as already mentioned. It suggests that research might fruitfully be directed at ascertaining whether or not there is a "critical mass" of elements, beyond which this mutual reinforcement by the individual elements takes hold to form a system. If so, then that minimal number (or set) of elements could be interpreted as indicating the threshold.

The second clue is the necessity for a *balance* of traits; e.g., both activism and a willingness to abide by decisions once made must be present in the minimal set; otherwise there will be too much activism, and the organization will be split apart (violating the first criterion, self-steering) or too much passivity and manipulation. Likewise, self-reliant traits must be accompanied by receptivity to the needs of others. These balancing sets show us what the organization cannot do without, and they thereby provide a second way to ascertain the minimum threshold.

Above this organizational threshold one meets the question of what constitutes the most *appropriate*, rather than just the minimally necessary, amount of participatory/democratic consciousness. The formal democratic ideology argues for an organization with only a minority of activists, leaving the rest of the membership to be passive and thus to provide the necessary stability (Almond and Verba, 1963). The radical-humanist ideology argues that this is insufficient, for it leaves the majority still not participating and, therefore, still not personally liberated. This latter ideological position in effect sets an individual threshold, as well as an organizational threshold. Its advocates consequently seek to foster the development of participatory/

democratic consciousness in as many individuals in the enterprise as possible (Myrdal, 1970; Macciochi, 1972).

Putting all of these considerations together, we may conclude at this point that although each individual does not need all the traits to participate, there is a qualitative minimum below which individuals become unable to give adequate support to democratization. This minimum can be estimated from the need for complementarity or balancing of certain tendencies, and by the mutually facilitating, systematic interrelationships of several traits.

At the company level, it is not necessary that all individuals be above their thresholds before democratization can begin. But certain individuals must have the consciousness well-developed, or there will not be democratic leadership among the rank-and-file nor democratizing behavior by company officials. Without these leaders, the authority function probably can still be carried out of course, but it will not be done democratically.

Growth or Decline of the Consciousness

What fosters and what inhibits or reverses the growth of this conscious-ness? Sometimes this consciousness appears to be a very delicate and vulnerable phenomenon, difficult to sustain without great, repeated efforts. Yugoslav practitioners frequently complain of the difficulty of sustaining it (Rus, 1973). The Cultural Revolution in China indicates what great efforts may be necessary to instill it (Myrdal, 1970). On the other hand, this mentality appears to have great durability once it has been firmly established in the minds of many people. In that condition it apparently can survive even long periods of non-democratic rule, as the experiences of Spanish anarchism and Czechoslovak reform movements testify (Dolgoff, 1973; Szulc, 1972). This seeming contradiction is explained by the fact that many of the elements of which this consciousness is composed are fundamental to the individual personality and therefore take a long time to acquire. (We have in mind, for instance, traits such as self-reliance or critical thinking.) By the same token, once such traits are acquired, their grounding in the basic personality allows them to persist for decades and, if incorporated into upbringing and daily practice in the home, even to be transmitted to the next generation.

Democratic consciousness can be fostered within the enterprise by the operation of the other five components. That is, once workers have a chance to have their demands transformed into company policy (component 1), are rewarded for extra output by a direct increase in their income (com-ponent 2), can obtain information about operations of the company that concern them (component 3), need no longer fear reprisals for speaking their mind (component 4), and have recourse to what they themselves regard as a fair appeals system in case of disputes with their supervisors (component 5), the traits of self-rule and resistance to manipulation have a chance to develop. They will not develop automatically, nor will every worker take the opportunity to become involved. But for those workers who already would like to have more input into how their jobs are run, the existence of the other five components creates the foundation on which their acquisition of the necessary traits can begin (see Figure 10.1 below).

Even if the worker's participation at the beginning is very small, research shows that this experience can reward him with increased self-confidence (Blumberg, 1968:Ch. 5 and 6), which is a crucial element in the self-governing consciousness.

Partial democratization does not inevitably grow to more complete forms; there are many points along the way where it may get stymied and fail. But it remains true that for a potentially large proportion of the work force, the experience of participation can begin the process of developing participatory/democratic consciousness (Pateman, 1970). This is true for managers as well as for workers. In companies that were transformed partially into democratization, managerial attitudes changed substantially toward a number of the values specified in Table 9.3. For example, managers in some Scanlon Plan firms evinced a much greater confidence in the ability and creativity of workers (power-holder's fourth trait) after seeing the suggestions and worker-initiated improvements that came forth over several years through the production and screening committees (McGregor, 1958). A similar change of attitude occurred among managers of plants partly democratized within Britain's huge Imperial Chemical Industries conglomerate (*Business Week*, 1970).

Such a transformation of attitudes by the operation of the other five components contributes one of the regenerative and reinforcing processes which are emphatically necessary if this delicate consciousness is to be maintained. Without such reinforcement from concrete behaviors associated with the other components, the consciousness component is not likely to be maintained at the level needed for effective democratization.

By the same token, the concrete experience of attempting democratization can discourage participants and move them away from the requisite attitudes, especially if any of the five earlier components is not present or is not functioning to a sufficient degree (beyond the minimal thresholds). Both parties then may become frustrated, and hostility can result. Distrust can arise between managers and managed (Number 5, Table 9.3) which will confirm to management the view that workers are incapable of contributing much of real value to company decision-making. Similarly, after such frustration, workers may move away from the activist stance into passivity (Number 9, Table 9.2), considering it more prudent to leave decisions in the hands of managers or, occasionally, also their unions.

Democratic consciousness can be reinforced or discouraged by factors outside the five components, as well. The external culture of the class, economy, or nation to which the firm's members belong can predispose them positively or negatively towards the values or traits that compose this consciousness. Such appears to have been the case for rural Spanish collectives which took root easily amongst a culture of primitive egalitarian Christianity, according to Gaston Leval (Dolgoff, 1974). This is also the case for the North American plywood cooperatives, which were initiated among an immigrant Scandinavian subculture with deep traditions of cooperation and frequent community practice of it through self-help organizations (Berman, 1967:Ch. 6).

Family upbringing and formal education also tend to equip individuals with the skills appropriate for democratic (or alternatively for authoritarian) modes of decision-making and conflict resolution (Anderson, 1971:Ch. 2, 3, 5). It is believed that these are carried over into one's place of work (Mulder, 1973).

External organizations that assume the training of workers and managers for democratization can imbue them with many of the requisite elements of participatory/democratic consciousness. Most often these have been militant labor organizations (as in Spain or Israel) or revolutionary political parties (as in China and Yugoslavia, [Dolgoff, 1974; Fine, 1973; Macciocchi, 1972; Hunnius, 1973]).

Finally, technology and the work-process it requires can condition a worker's consciousness toward servility or toward self-expression and self-management. Blauner found that craft industries (like printing) and continuous-process work (like petro-chemical operations) are conducive to participatory consciousness. On the other hand, machine-tending jobs and assembly-line work tend to breed attitudes of cynicism, low self-esteem, and fear—attitudes which would inhibit the worker from taking part in democratization (Blauner, 1964:43, 64–70, 80, 176–178; Pateman, 1970; Lipset, 1961).

The fact that participatory consciousness is so susceptible to these external forces has led some persons to argue that democratization of enterprises will be a hopeless aim until the surrounding society is changed in a participatory direction first. But there is much evidence to show that external factors need not predominate over the internal consciousness of a democratized firm. They are but conditioning influences which can facilitate or burden the otherwise relatively autonomous company mentality. Persuasive demonstration of this fact comes from the several cases of democratized firms operating in environments which are much less participatory than they; such cases form the bulk of Part I of this study. An even stronger indication comes from the fact that individual members of some democratized firms tend to take a more active, participatory role in their surrounding communities (Blum, 1968; Walton, 1974b; McWhinney in Jenkins, 1973:244). It appears the net flow of consciousness in these cases is from the more participatory work situation outward into the less participatory environment. The environment has not prevented the outward flow nor has it effectively suppressed participatory consciousness in such firms.

10

Overview of the Components in Interaction

Having delved into the nature of each component and having explored the range of forms they each manifest, we can now bring them together for an overall look. Figure 10.1 does this graphically, focusing on one major feedback system of the six components—the individual employee's willingness to participate. Other foci could have been selected—such as the interactions of the six components on employees' wage desires, or on managers' expectations about workers' abilities—but for purposes of illustration just one focus was used. This particular focus was chosen because willingness to participate is acknowledged by several other authors to be crucial to the overall success or failure of democratization (Mulder, 1971; Rus, 1973; Fine, 1973).

Our model enables us to identify several causes of change in this crucial factor. Beginning in the upper, right-hand quadrant of the model, the basic components are arranged clockwise (each within a double-lined, circular space). Each component is regarded as satisfying a specific condition crucial to the motivation of employees to continue participating. In the diagram, these conditions are posed as questions: "Is one or another means available?" Each such question is presented in a rectangular space directly preceding the component. For example, in the upper right-hand rectangle: "I. Does there exist means for getting one's views frequently into decision-making bodies?" If the component is present and functioning, then the question is answered in the affirmative (Yes: direct participation or elected representation) and the condition is being satisfied within that particular company's system of work democratization.

The consequences of each component's activity are then diagrammed feeding forward by raising the need for other conditions (e.g., Rectangle II: "Are there any tangible rewards to the participant for his/her extra effort . . . ?" in lower, right-hand corner of the model). Or the consequences are seen to feed backward, reinforcing the employee's willingness to participate again (long arrows around border of model culminating at the circle of High willingness to participate in component 6).

If the component is not present or is not functioning, then the condition posed is not being satisfied in a particular case. The consequences of its absence are followed along feedbacks through the NO boxes to various depressing effects on the employee's willingness to participate further. Those effects (portrayed in the large, double-lined central box of the model, within component 6) can range from mere caution and frustration, to fear, accumulated resentment, and cynicism. After a while, these conditions lead to long-term apathy and a probable withdrawal from participation, which is indicated in the center of component 6 receding behind the Low or None position.

Let us follow these flows one at a time. Taking a developmental perspective, we start with the first active degree of participation that may occur in a real-life situation, even in the most minor and partial forms of workplace democratization. This occurs when employees offer a criticism or suggestion intended to affect or change a policy of the firm (arrow from top center to top right of Figure 10.1). If they are at least willing to try that initial step, there still needs to be some recognizable channel to which they can bring the suggestion or criticism. If there is—i.e., if the alternative stated in the upper right-hand rectangle (I) exists in the affirmative—then some form of component 1 is present (direct or representative participation, indicated in the upper right-hand circle). Employee willingness to make an approach then combines with this open channel to yield the action of participation (right-side large oval: Participation Attempted). If the employees' suggestions are not adopted, they may feel frustrated and may cease trying to participate any further (feedback line into component 6, center of model, via frustration). A few employees, however, may be spurred on by the initial setback to try harder a second time (dotted line through first-time frustration to high willingness).

If employee suggestions or criticisms are adopted, on the other hand, they are very likely to feel uplifted. And their willingness to try participation a second time is made much more likely (feedback through intrinsic reward of success).

After the first experience, the factor of iteration begins to play a decisive role (indicated by the counter-and-memory function in small oval, right-side of chart between the alternatives of Not Adopted and Adopted). For example, if the employee's suggestions or criticisms are *repeatedly* rejected, frustration or disappointment are likely to turn into cynicism and apathy; withdrawal from further attempts at participation becomes likely. (See arrow labelled Many Times, linking the negative side of the counter-memory to component 6. Repeated disappointments are of course a recognized procedure for extinction of behaviors (Hebb, 1949) and such would be the result of a series of rejections of employee attempts at participation.

In a similar manner, repeated positive adoption of employee ideas has decisive consequences. After several adoptions of their suggestions, some employees may begin to ask what they are "getting out of it" (condition listed in rectangle II in the lower right-hand corner) since they see that at least some of their suggestions have involved ways to prevent waste of materials, time, or energy on their job and thereby have aided the company materially. Employees for whom that becomes a concern are likely to experience resentment if they are refused tangible rewards (line from NO by II, to Resentment in component 6), and that resentment can in turn lead them to reduce future efforts to make suggestions or constructive criticisms (line to Low or None in willingness to participate).

If, on the other hand, the alternative posed in this second rectangle is answered in the affirmative ("Yes: frequent return . . ."; see large circle, bottom right of diagram), then the second necessary component is present,

Figure 10.1

INTERACTION OF THE COMPONENTS

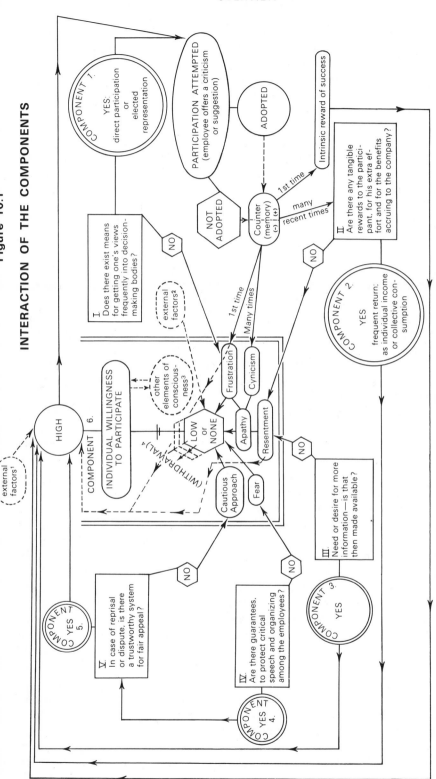

Notes:

1. External factors that promote higher willingness to participate are, for example: (a) direct encouragement of participation by union, management, or militant party; (b) high levels of education, of skill; (c) substantial contact with a participatory culture.

2. External factors which inhibit or discourage willingness to participate: e.g., (a) generally authoritarian upbringing (b) routine, repetitive jobs.

3. Other elements of consciousness that can predispose a person towards or away from attempting participation. Columns II & III in Table 9.2 show the elements that predispose one towards; and columns I & IV, those that predispose one away from participation.

4. One route out of this plane of concerns to other possible actions—e.g., absenteeism, demands for higher compensation.

and the employee's willingness to continue to participate actively tends to be reinforced (feedback loop from component 2 to high willingness).

An occasion can arise when in order to formulate a proposal, employees will feel they need more information (or even have been told by managers that they do). If they cannot obtain access to that information (alternative posed in Rectangle III), they are likely to feel resentful (line from NO into component 6). Some employees may be spurred on by such a setback, as we saw earlier with component 1 when a criticism was not initially adopted. Such employees' motivation to try a second time may actually increase from this first disappointment (dotted arrow leading from resentment to high willingness within component 6). But others will turn apathetic from such a rebuff (illustrated by the oval, apathy, above resentment), especially after several occasions of such rebuff. These employees may then decide that it is useless to participate on most issues of importance to them. That is not to say disappointed employees will cease participation altogether; rather they will become discouraged to a certain extent, and their motivation to participate will drop (the central hexagon therefore states the case of LOW willingness, not just the absolute NONE).

If, by contrast, the desired information is obtainable, then the third necessary component is operating (see circle to the left of rectangle III); and the employees not only can utilize it to complete their participation this time, but are likely to feel positively oriented towards participation generally (the feedback line from component 3 to an increase in willingness).

An important consideration if one's contribution is a criticism—not just an innocent suggestion—is to know whether or not one will be protected against reprisal from those one's criticism is to reflect upon (see alternative IV, the left-most rectangle). If such guarantees do not exist, employees are less likely to risk participation (indicated by line from NO through Fear to low or no willingness). If there are such guarantees, including an appeals system for settling disputes when the criticized person(s) attempt a reprisal (condition V—top left rectangle), then the fourth and fifth necessary components are present and participation is likely to continue (feedback line from component 5 to high willingness). If the guarantees and trustworthy appeal system are not present, the employee can be expected to proceed cautiously—if at all (see feedbacks through Cautious Approach and Fear in component 6).

Regarded as a whole, the interdependence of the components operates through a positive or reinforcing cycle and a negative or extinguishing cycle. The negative cycle (inner portion of the chart) is entered if any of the initial five components are absent, or if experience confronts employees with too many rejections of their attempts at participation. The positive reinforcement cycle (outer portion of the chart) is entered when each of the five initial components are added (and so long as they continue to function effectively), as well as when experience rewards the employees with adoptions of their suggestions and criticisms.

The model reveals the important fact of *simultaneity* in the dynamics of workplace management. Some past attempts at democratizing the workplace have failed because their implementors failed to realize this need and did not introduce enough components at once. At other times failure occurred because the implementors assumed that attention to one component was sufficient when in reality the readjustment or coordination of several components at once is required.

Of course, feedback from the five outer components is not the sole condition affecting an individual's willingness to participate. Other elements of consciousness within the sixth component, as well as external factors, can increase or decrease the employee's willingness, as shown in the chart and as previously discussed. Also it must be emphasized that there is an external region beyond the Low Willingness or None hexagon into which an employee's motivation may flow as a result of the cynicism engendered by disappointment on this plane of affairs. That external realm includes actions such as absenteeism, slowdowns, sabotage, wage demands, and wildcat strikes. In other words, the Low Willingness or None should not be misinterpreted as always indicating a dead-end—that no *other* action is taken by employees. It indicates solely that they do not take action to *participate* in existing channels or to broaden those channels and add components. Apathetic, cynical, resentful employees may indeed act in ways that affect the company. But those ways lie outside of democratic participation in management and, therefore, outside of this chart. Significantly, such actions have been observed to decrease when democratization is instituted and to increase again when it is taken away (Blumberg, 1968; Potvin, 1958).

It should be emphasized once more that this is only one set of linkages of the six components, the set that bears most directly on employee willingness to offer suggestions or criticisms. There are certainly other linkages among these components which should be examined closely by further research.

11

Summary, Conclusions, and Research Prospects

In this study we have considered a wide range of empirical cases of workplace democratization—spanning several countries, ideological systems, and degrees of democratization. Included in that set are several worker-owned and worker-managed firms in the United States which we investigated first-hand. Utilizing that broad data base we were able to begin answering questions that are basic to the field: what is necessary for successful, ongoing democratization of the workplace? And what are democratization's principal sources of failure? Our strategy was to seek the *minimal* number of components that could account for the maintenance and success of democratization in a profit-making firm.

For the present, the analysis has been confined to factors internal to the firm, which proved to be sufficiently complex for the scope of a single study. We found that separating internal from external factors for the purposes of analysis was conceptually feasible and was not seriously challenged by the case material. Yet the model generated herein was kept open to—and appears quite capable of extension to—include these external factors. Indeed, that is one of our goals for subsequent research.

The primary focus in this study was political: the issues of management, power, and decision-making within the firm. Economic questions were not neglected, but we confined our analysis to those that most directly bear on the question of worker-manager relations (e.g., wages, productivity, creation and distribution of the surplus). Psychological factors emerged as crucial to certain parts of the management process and so were given due consideration, especially since workers' motivation to participate emerged as a central link between factors conditioning success or failure of democratization in the workplace. Though we were concerned with workers' motivation, this was not a study in the tradition of worker satisfaction and dissatisfaction that has evolved in contemporary social psychology (e.g., Smith et al., 1969; Brayfield and Rothe, 1951 Herzberg et al., 1959). Finally, our primary focus on political interactions meant that we gave little attention to technical factors affecting the work-process and the worker's situation within that process.

The method of our study was to integrate the vast case literature by constructing an inductive model. We aimed to keep the model as simple as possible, while developing it with contrasting case material in order to make it as inclusive as possible. Four criteria were employed to delimit the region the model would have to fill: systemic viability, economic viability, democratic and humanizing processes of management (pages 8–9).

With these criteria governing our analysis of case material, we identified the following components as minimally necessary for workplace democratization:

1.   Participation in decision-making,
2.   Economic return to the participants based on the surplus they produce,
3.   Sharing management-level information with employees,
4.   Guaranteed individual rights,
5.   An independent appeals system, and
6.   A complex participatory/democratic consciousness.

Together, these six components and their interactions comprise our first stage model, the major finding of this study. It turns out that without any one of these components, the employees' willingness to participate is difficult to maintain. Their firm, thus, is unlikely to experience democratic management for very long. Even though the structure be formally democratic, it is unlikely that actual democratic participation by the employees will take place if one or more of the six components is absent. In cases where democratic participation is already active, the removal of one or more of these six components (or their gradual decline in function) usually leads to a gradual withdrawal of employees from participation until the democratic format becomes mostly illusory. At that point the management function still survives, but in an oligarchic form with little or no feedback from below.

After identifying these six fundamental components and some of their major interactions and effects on the firm, the nature of each one of the components was studied. We found that participation, individual rights, and consciousness have the most complex internal composition. Participation possesses several dimensions or characteristics operating simultaneously, and they are found in many different combinations in empirical cases. Individual rights and consciousness each are composed of several discrete elements which need to operate together as a coherent system if they are to be thoroughly effective. The other three components, information-sharing, economic return, and a just appeals system were discovered to be complex in another way: the basic principles by which they operate are subtle and frequently accompanied by ideological controversy.

It was found that each component can be realized empirically by a wide spectrum of forms, yet only some of these forms are effective in sustaining democratization. We, therefore, pressed our analysis further, in order to ascertain the precise thresholds where each component begins to contribute to the maintenance of workplace democratization. These thresholds were not defined *a priori* but were induced from the data of successful and unsuccessful instances of democratization. For certain components, such as consciousness, it is not yet possible to specify an exact minimum threshold. Nevertheless, it was possible to derive indications of the likely characteristics of its threshold.

Our research led also to the generation of certain hypothetical forms for a few of the components, forms that have not yet appeared in concrete cases (to our knowledge) but which follow the basic principles uncovered for that component. An example of this is found in our analysis of the independent judicial system (pp. 85–86).

The six-component model is a developmental one, reflecting that the lack of one or more of these six components forces a choice upon the firm. Either the firm must alter the system and adopt a new component— the relevant missing one(s) —to give the employees more rights and power; or the firm may abort the attempt at democratization because management is unwilling to accept any expansion of workers' power, or because the workers themselves do not feel capable of taking on more responsibility and power.

Although the consciousness of managers is considered a crucial element in the model, our finding generally was that the consciousness of the employees was more critical in the long run, especially their motivation to participate. This motivation proved to be affected by each of the other five necessary components, according to their fluctuations and presence or absence. Democratization cannot function well until the workers themselves want it. This seems obvious, but the point has often been ignored. The experience of newly independent countries reminds us, in a different context, that it does little good to set up democratic structures (even with democratically minded leaders) if the public itself is not ready to act according to the new, democratic set of rules. So even if it were possible to obtain democratically minded managers for a firm, the problem would remain of how to motivate the workers to take part. The findings of the present research suggests that several variables are required, operating simultaneously within certain specified ranges.

How does this model compare with others that deal with power and participation in work organizations? Briefly, it appears to be compatible with many other models, yet distinct from them; for example, the study of relations between employees, supervisors, and higher-level management assembled by Tannenbaum and Cooke (1974) cites many findings which support the present model. Their evidence on leadership styles (Tannenbaum and Cooke, 1974:38–40) supports this model's treatment of the consciousness most suitable for power-holders (Table 9.3) and the general membership (Table 9.2). On the other hand, their assertion that managers can increase their control at the same time as workers increase their control over the same operation would seem at first to contradict our conceptualization of Dimension I, the degree of control exercised by workers in each form of participatory decision-making (Figure 4.1). Further examination shows that Tannenbaum and Cooke themselves have reservations about whether *actual* control was measured by the instruments used (Tannenbaum and Cooke, 1974:36–37; 43–44) or only the participants' perceived spheres of access. If the latter is the case, their findings would be compatible with our own generalizations.

Another model, March and Simon's (1958), has parallels to the present one but covers a separate territory. Employee participation in its terms refers only to laboring and attendance, not to participation in decision-making which is the focus of our model. Since their model was abstracted from conventional managerial organizations and not from democratized organizations, it describes the management function as belonging to a separate class of managers (March and Simon, 1958:90), not to the rank-and-file, or to persons selected by the rank-and-file or held explicitly accountable by them, the thresholds in our model. Yet on general organizational processes, such as the nature of decision-making itself, the two models could probably find much overlap. To contemplate developing the present model in that direction raises the general question of further research, to which we now turn.

Several avenues of research are open for further development and use of the model. The dimensions of participation uncovered in the course of our analysis—such as the degree of employee influence, the range of issues over which that influence is exercised, and the organizational level at which it is exercised seem capable of further development into reliable scales. Were they so developed, these scales could improve comparative analysis of case studies by increasing the precision with which cases are classified and analyzed. Even before developing such scales, we have seen that bringing two or more of the dimensions to bear on specific cases illuminates previously confused issues. Cases can be compared with greater understanding and less subjectivity than before. (See, for example, Figures 4.4, 4.5, and 4.10.)

At this stage in its development, the model suggests several propositions we would like to test out against new empirical cases. We have already gathered a list of firms which practice various degrees of democratization and which were not utilized here. These new cases can provide the necessary fresh data base against which to test the model's implications. In so doing it will be possible to move from the inductive phase to the deductive. Propositions already being derived from the model will have to be transformed into testable hypotheses. Of major interest in this regard are the patterns of dynamic development from one form of democratization to another.

For similar reasons, the conditions of stabilization at any particular form should be explored. We wish to know more precisely what mechanisms and conditions are influential in containing, neutralizing, or balancing the dynamic tendencies so that stabilization occurs. It is reasonable to suspect that, besides a complex balance of forces, an especially important factor for stability is the sixth component, the participants' consciousness. This variable is difficult to measure precisely, but because of its central role a concerted attempt at refined measurement is well worth the effort.

Another important avenue of research is to inquire which other components might be necessary for democratization and should be added to the model. Certainly other elements besides the six developed in the present study play important roles in many democratized workplaces. We did examine them but did not bring them into the model because the evidence so far did not demonstrate them to be indispensable to democratization. However, in the next stage of research it might be advantageous to decide to modify the criteria of selection in order to add to the model components which facilitate or advance democratization even though not essential to its basic survival. At the moment, prime candidates for such additions are:

1. Job-equalization
2. Status-equalization
3. Pay-equalization
4. Forbidding individual rewards, in favor of collective consumption, and
5. Abolishing private ownership.

The first three practices—equalization of jobs, status, and pay—facilitate, accelerate, or deepen democratization because they can reinforce the sixth component, consciousness. Rotation of jobs (which is one way of realizing the job-equalization principle) can foster attitudes of reciprocity and equality, in particular, attitudes which we found necessary for power-holders in a democratized firm (Table 9.3). The Chinese practice of requiring doctors and teachers to work in fields and factories is one example (Macciochi, 1973); the rotation of persons between menial and managerial jobs within the Israeli kibbutz is another (Tabb and Goldfarb, 1970).

Equalization of pay—whereby all members receive the same pay regardless of their task—goes even further in erasing distinctions among participants. Differences of skill and responsibility are no longer taken as sufficient reason for differences in personal income. The abolition of economic distinctions is seen as removing an interference from human relations and hence is regarded as an additional step toward realization of the humanization criterion associated with democratization.

In a similar vein, some collectives think it is better to distribute the surplus (that economic return which is above the regular wage) in a group form rather than as payment to individuals. Community improvements such as recreation halls are common examples of this form of distribution in Yugoslavia and China (Blumberg, 1968; Myrdal, 1970). The argument behind this practice is that individual payments weaken the consciousness component. They break down group identity and group concern and foster selfish motives with individualist orientations, which can interfere with the group activities required for participatory enterprise and society. An argument in response to that assertion, however, would hold that the experience of joint decision-making and coordinated production are much more fundamental to attitude formation than whatever form the payments may take, especially if they are made only annually or quarterly from profits.

A more far-reaching element is encountered with the question of ownership. Many persons have argued that worker control cannot exist without worker-ownership (Lichtheim, 1970). Nevertheless, it is true that substantial democratization does occur in firms which are owned privately by absentee stockholders (e.g., Scanlon Plan companies). There are also the opposite cases where workers own their own company but exercise little real control (e.g., ACIPCO)*. Furthermore, if one argues that ownership must not be in private hands for democratization to be assured, one needs to specify which kinds of alternate ownership are being recommended. A number of competing possibilities are available, each with disadvantages

---

* Pages 36–39.

and advantages, and each therefore requiring a great deal of further research. Besides ownership by the workers themselves, there can be ownership by the community through the state (as in the USSR, Brinton; 1970, or in Canadian provinces, Shearer, 1974); ownership by the local populace through an elected assembly (as in communitarian cases, Tabb and Goldfarb, 1970); ownership by voluntary citizen purchase of shares (as in several Black community development organizations in America, Hampden-Turner, 1974). One can even attempt the complete absence of ownership by anyone, as "social ownership" is defined to be in Yugoslavia (Adizes, 1971). There, the discrete functions associated with ownership are so dispersed among several different parties that no single party can be located as "owner" nor, theoretically, can a single party exert enough rights to act alone as owner.

The root of the matter regarding ownership seems to lie with the recognition that ownership is not a single factor but rather a bundle of several discrete functions and rights (Dahl, 1970). Ownership is more than just legal title to some property. It involves also control over the use of the property, i.e., its management. It involves the right to dispose of (sell or donate) the property. It consists also of first claim on any income accrued through use of the property (e.g., profits from capital used in production).

Yet already the prerogatives of managing and receiving profits are partly included in our six elements of democratization. Control over use of the property is shared with the workers as soon as component 1 takes effect (participation in decision-making). Given the general trend whereby many ownership functions have passed to professional managers in today's companies (Berle and Means, 1932; Galbraith, 1967), democratization's transfer of some management powers to the employees is likely to simul-taneously transfer some functions of ownership. The owner's traditional claim on income accrued through use of the property is also exercised by workers in democratized firms, as soon as component 2 is instituted (economic return from the surplus above wages).

Several other elements of the ownership relation, however, are not included so far among our six components. One is the ultimate right to dispose of the assets of the firm. It is with such questions that we would like to begin further research. We feel that it is more advantageous to treat the complex phenomenon of ownership in each of its constituent parts, rather than to treat it as if it were a single component, as do some democrati-zation movements (e.g. strict Marxists). Our research may ultimately come to the conclusion already held by them: that private ownership sets too low a limit on the opportunities for meaningful democratization. But even then our analysis would remain open to examine several alternatives to private ownership besides state ownership—for example, communitarian ownership, dispersed social ownership, worker or cooperative ownership, and so forth. Ownership is too complex a phenomenon to be brought into or excluded from the model as a single component. Some of its functions are already included, and others deservingly claim high priority for attention in the next stage of research.

REFERENCES

Adizes, Ichak. *Industrial Democracy: Yugoslav Style.* NY: Columbia University
1973   Press.
————. "Role of Management in Democratic (Communal) Organization,"
1971   *Annals of Public and Cooperative Economy,* 42:399–420.
Agenor: European Review (Brussels) No. 13. "Industrial Democracy," 28–40.
1969
Almond, Gabriel A., and Sidney Verba. *The Civic Culture: Political Attitudes and*
1963   *Democracy in Five Nations.* Princeton: Princeton University Press.
American Friends Service Committee (ed.). *Democratizing the Workplace: From*
1973   *Job Enrichment to Workers' Control.* Cambridge: AFSC.
Anderson, C. H. *Toward a New Sociology—A Critical View.* Homewood, Ill.:
1971   Dorsey Press.
Argyris, Chris. *Human Behavior in Organizations.* NY: Harper and Row.
1954

————. "Organizational Leadership and Participative Management," *The Journal*
1966   *of Business,* 28 (January): 1–7.
Barratt-Brown, Michael. "Alternative Structures for Mining Industry," *Workers*
1975   *Control Bulletin,* No. 30 (December): 8–9.
Beer, Stafford. *Decision and Control: The Meaning of Operational Research and*
1966   *Management Cybernetics.* London: John Wiley and Sons.
Behn, William, Martin Carnoy, Joyce Crain, and Henry Levin. *Educational Require-*
1976   *ments for Industrial Democracy.* Palo Alto, Calif.: Center for Economic
    Studies.
Bellas, Carl J. *Industrial Democracy and the Worker-Owned Firm: A Study of*
1972   *Twenty-One Plywood Companies in the Pacific Northwest.* NY: Praeger.
Benello, C. George. "Implementing Self-Management in the United States: The
1975   Funding and Educational Development Organization." Ithaca, N.Y.:
    F.E.D.O., Mimeographed.
Bentley, Walter L. "Organization and Procedures of the American Cast Iron
1925   Company." Master's Thesis, Department of Commerce and Administration,
    University of Chicago.
Bergnéhr, Bo. "Secrecy Regulations Under the New Act of Collective Bargaining."
1975   Remarks delivered at the Symposium on Swedish Collective Bargaining
    Legislation, Institute of Industrial Relations, University of California, Los
    Angeles, October 8–9. Mimeographed.
Berman, Katrina V. *Worker-Owned Plywood Companies, An Economic Analysis.*
1967   Pullman: Washington State University Press.
Bernstein, Harry. "Democracy on the Job: Grand Goal in Sweden." *Los Angeles*
1974   *Times.* November 9: 1, 24, 25.
Bernstein, Paul. "Existing Democratized Enterprises in the U.S. and Britain."
1973   In *Democratizing the Workplace: From Job Enrichment to Worker's
    Control.* Cambridge, Mass.: American Friends Service Committee, 1–13.
————. "Worker-Owned Plywood Companies of the Pacific Northwest,"
1974   *Working Papers for a New Society,* 2 (Summer): 24–36.
Bernstein, Paul, and Marjorie Young. "Democratic Mentality in the Czechoslovak
1973   Reform Movement." Mimeographed.
Bettelheim, Charles. *Cultural Revolution and Industrial Organization in China.*
1974   NY: Monthly Review Press.
Blauner, Robert. *Alienation and Freedom.* Chicago: University of Chicago Press.
1964

Bloss, Esther.   *Labor Legislation in Czechoslovakia.* NY: Columbia University Press.
1938

Blum, Fred H.   *Work and Community: The Scott-Bader Commonwealth and the*
1968   *Quest for a New Social Order.* London: Routledge and Kegan Paul.

Blumberg, Paul.   *Industrial Democracy: The Sociology of Participation.* NY: Schocken
1968   Books.

Blumenthal, W. Michael.   *Co-determination in the German Steel Industry.* Princeton:
1956   Princeton University Press.

Brant, Irving.   *The Bill of Rights: Its History and Meaning.* NY: Collier.
1964

Brayfield, Arthur, and Harold F. Rothe.   "An Index of Job Satisfaction." *Journal*
1951   *of Applied Psychology,* 35 (October): 307–311.

Brinton, Maurice.   *The Bolsheviks and Workers' Control, 1917–1921: The State*
1970   *and Counter Revolution.* London: Solidarity.

Brown, Douglas V.   "Problems Under the Scanlon Plan: Summary-Management
1958   Session." In Lesieur, 1958.

Burns, Tom, and G. M. Stalker.   *The Management of Innovation.* London: Tavistock
1961   Publications.

Business Week.   "Getting at the Root of a Labor Crisis." October 17: 56–59.
1970

Business Week.   "Managing Alberta's Oil Money." March 31: 76–77.
1975

Čekota, Anthony.   "Thomas Bat'a—Pioneer of Self-Government in Industry."
1964   In Miroslav Rechcigl (ed.), *The Czechoslovak Contribution to to World*
       Culture. The Hague: Mouton, 342:349.

Clegg, Hugh A.   *Industrial Democracy and Nationalization.* Oxford: Basil Blackwell.
1955

————.   *A New Approach to Industrial Democracy.* London: Blackwell.
1960

Clegg, Ian.   *Workers' Self-Management in Algeria.* London: Allen Lane, the Penguin
1971   Press.

Coates, Ken (ed.).   *Can the Workers Run Industry?* London: Sphere Books, Ltd.
1968a

Coates, Ken, and Tony Topham.   "Participation or Control?" in Ken Coates 1968a.
1968b

Cole, G. D. H.   *Socialist Thought: The Forerunners, 1789–1850.* London: Macmillan.
1967

Dahl, Henry G.   *Worker-Owned Plywood Companies in the State of Washington.*
1957   Everett, Wash.: First National Bank of Everett, April. Uncirculated.

Dahl, Robert A.   *After the Revolution: Authority in a Good Society.* New Haven,
1970   Conn.: Yale University Press.

————.   *Modern Political Analysis.* Englewood Cliffs, NJ: Prentice-Hall.
1963

————.   "Power to the Worker?" *New York Review of Books,* 15:9.
1970

Das, Napagopal.   *Experiments in Industrial Democracy.* Bombay: Asia Publishing
1964   House.

Davis, Louis E., Albert Cherns, and Associates.   *Quality of Working Life.* (New York:
1975   Free Press,) 2 Vols.

DeGreene, Kenyon B.   *Sociotechnical Systems: Factors in Analysis, Design, and*
1973   *Management.* Englewood Cliffs, NJ.: Prentice-Hall, Inc.

Denitch, B.   "On the Relevance of Yugoslav Self-Management," *Participation*
1973   *and Self-Management,* 6 Zagreb: Institute for Social Research.

Derber, Milton.   *The American Idea of Industrial Democracy, 1965–1965.* Chicago:
1970   University of Illinois Press.

Derrick, Paul, and J. F. Phipps (eds.).   *Co-ownership, Co-operation, and Control:*
1969   *An Industrial Objective.* London: Longmans, Green and Co.

Deutsch, Karl W. *The Analysis of International Relations.* Englewood Cliffs, N.J.:
1968   Prentice-Hall.
——————. *Nerves of Government: Models of Political Communication and*
1963   *Control.* Glencoe, Ill: The Free Press.
Dolgoff, Sam (ed.). *The Anarchist Collectives: Workers' Self-Management in*
1974   *the Spanish Revolution 1936–1939.* Montreal: Black Rose Books.
Douglas, Paul H. "Shop Committees: Substitute for, or Supplement to, Trade
1921   Unions?" *Journal of Political Economy,* 29 (February): 89–107.
Dubin, Robert. "Theory Building in Applied Areas," in Marvin D. Dunnette (ed.),
1975   *Handbook of Industrial Psychology.* Chicago: Rand McNally.
Dubreuil, Hyacinthe. *L'exemple de Bata: La libération des initiatives individuelles*
1963   *dans une entreprise géante.* Paris: Grasset, 5th ed.
Dunlop, John T. "Political Systems and Industrial Relations," *International Institute*
1973   *of Labour Studies Bulletin,* Geneva 9:115.
Dunn, William. "The Economics of Organizational Ideology," *International Socio-*
1973   *logical Conference on Participation and Self-Management,* 6. Zagreb:
        Institute for Social Research.
Dyer, Lee. "Implications of New Theories of Work for the Design of Compensation
1975   Systems," Ithaca, N.Y.: N.Y. State School of Industrial and Labor Relations.
        Mimeographed.
Eckstein, Harry. "A Theory of Stable Democracy," in *Division and Cohesion in*
1966   *Democracy.* Princeton: Princeton University Press, Appendix B.
Emery, Frederick, and Einar Thorsrud. *Form and Content in Industrial Democracy.*
1969   London: Tavistock.
Emery, Frederick E., and Eric L. Trist. "Socio-Technical Systems." In F. E. Emery (ed.):
1969   *Systems Thinking.* NY: Vintage. 281–296.
Employees' Manual. Birmingham, Alabama: American Cast Iron Pipe Co.
1969
Fairley, Lincoln. *The Company Union in Plan and Practice.* NY: Affiliated Schools
1936   for Workers.
Farrow, Nigel. "John Lewis Partnership: the Profit in Worker-Ownership," *Business*
1964   (Sept.), Reprinted in Paul Derrick and J. F. Phipps (eds.), *Co-ownership,*
        Co-operation, and Control. London: Longman's Green, 1968:83–91.
——————. "Scott-Bader Commonwealth, Ltd." *Business* (Jan.) Reprinted in
1965   Derrick, 1969:95–100.
Fein, Mitchell. *Wage Incentive Plans.* Work Methods and Measurement Division
1970   Publication No. 2. New York: American Institute of Industrial Engineers.
Fibich, Jindrich. *Bureaucracy and Bureaucratism.* Trans. Richard Correll and Paul
1967   Bernstein, forthcoming. Czech original: *K otázkám byrokracie a byrokratismu.*
        Prague: Academia Press.
Fine, Keitha S. "Workers' Participation in Israel," in Hunnius, 1973b.
1973
Flaes, Robert B. "Yugoslavian Experience of Workers' Self-Management," *Inter-*
1973   *national Sociological Conference on Participation and Self-Management,*
        6. Zagreb: Institute for Social Research, pp. 113–122.
Flanders, Allan, Ruth Pomeranz, and Joan Woodward. *Experiment in Industrial*
1968   *Democracy: A Study of the John Lewis Partnership.* London: Faber and
        Faber.
Freire, Paulo. *Education for Critical Consciousness.* NY: Seabury Press.
1974
——————. *Pedagogy of the Oppressed.* NY: Seabury Press.
1970
French, J. R. P., J. Israel, and D. Aas. "An Experiment in Participation in a Norwegian
1960   Factory," *Human Relations,* 13: 3–10.
French, J. R. P., and B. Raven. "Bases of Social Power," in D. Cartwright (ed.)
1959   *Studies in Social Power.* Ann Arbor, Mich: University of Michigan Press,
        150–167.

Frost, Carl, et al. *The Scanlon Plan for Organizational Development.* East Lansing: Michigan State University Press.

Garson, G. David. "Definitions and Distinctions Pertaining to Work Democratiza-
1974   tion." Paper presented to First National Conference of People for Self-Management. MIT, January. Mimeographed.

Gorupić, Drago, and I. Paj. "Workers' Participation in Management in Yugoslavia."
1971   *International Institute of Labour Studies Bulletin* 9:129–172.

Gorz, André. *Strategy for Labor: A Radical Proposal.* Trans. Martin A. Nicolaus and
1967   Victoria Ortiz. Boston: Beacon Press.

Gouldner, Alvin. *Patterns of Industrial Bureaucracy.* NY: Free Press.
1954

Greenberg, Edward S. "Consequences of Worker Participation & Control: A
1975   Clarification of the Theoretical Literature." *Social Science Quarterly* (September).

Gustavsen, Bjorn. "Environmental Requirements and the Democratization of
1973   Industrial Organizations." *International Sociological Conference on Participation and Self-Management,* 4:5–22.

Hackman, J. Richard. "The Coming Demise of Work Redesign," *Harvard Business*
1975   *Review,* (July/August).

Hampden-Turner, Charles. *From Poverty to Dignity: A Strategy for Poor Americans.*
1974   Garden City, NY: Anchor Press/Doubleday.

Hebb, Donald O. *The Organization of Behavior.* New York: Wiley.
1949

Heller, F. A., and J. B. Rose. "Participation in Decision-Making Re-examined."
1973   In *International Sociological Conference on Participation and Self-Management* 4. Zagreb: Institute for Social Research, 123–124.

Herman, Peter. "Workers, Watches, and Self-management," *Working Papers*
1974   *for a New Society,* I (Winter): 18–25.

Herzberg, Frederick, Bernard Mauser, and Barbara Bloch Snyderman. *The Motivation*
1959   *to Work.* New York: John Wiley & Sons.

HEW. U.S. Department of Health Education and Welfare, *Work in America.*
1973   Cambridge: MIT Press.

Hindus, Maurice. *The Bright Passage.* NY: Doubleday & Co.
1947

Holloway, Mark. *Heavens on Earth: Utopian Communities in America.* NY: Dover.
1960

Horvat, Branko, and Vlado Raskovic. "Workers Management in Yugoslavia,"
1959   *Journal of Political Economy,* 47 (April).

Hunnius, Gerry. "Workers' Self-Management in Yugoslavia." In Hunnius, 1973b:
1973a   268–321.

Hunnius, Gerry, G. David Garson, and John Case (eds.). *Workers' Control: A*
1973b   *Reader on Labor and Social Change.* NY: Random House.

Hurst, Ronald. "We Have No Strikes," *Scotland* (June) unpaginated; reprint
1971   available from Scott-Bader Ltd., Wollaston, Northamptonshire, NN9 7RL, England.

International Labor Office. "The Bat'a Boot and Shoe Factory," *Studies on Industrial*
1930   *Relations: Studies and Reports Series A,* 33:217–263.

International Sociological Conference on Participation and Self-Management.
1972–73   6 Vols. Zagreb, Yugoslavia: Institute for Social Research.

Jenkins, David. *Job Power: Blue and White Collar Democracy.* Garden City, N.J:
1973   Doubleday and Company.

Karlsson, Lars Erik. "Experiments in Industrial Democracy in Sweden," *International*
1973   *Sociological Conference on Participation and Self-Management,* 3. Zagreb: Institute for Social Research: 71–102.

Kasindorf, Jean. "England: Revolt in a Shoe Factory," in American Friends Service
1973   Comm. (ed.) 1973.

Kmetić, M. *Self-Management in the Enterprise.* Belgrade.
1967

Kolaja, Jiři. *A Polish Factory: A Case Study in Workers' Participation*. London:
1960   Lexington.
—————. *Workers' Councils: The Yugoslav Experience*. London: Tavistock.
1965
Kovanda, Karel. "Workers' Control in Czechoslovakia 1968–1970." Ph.D. Disserta-
1974   tion: Department of Political Science, Massachusetts Institute of
         Technology.
Lauck, W. Jett. *Political Democracy and Industrial Democracy*. NY: Funk and
1926   Wagnalls.
Lesieur, Frederick G. (ed.). *The Scanlon Plan: A Frontier in Labor-Management
1958   Cooperation*. Cambridge: MIT Press.
Lichtheim, George. *The Origins of Socialism*. NY: Frederick A. Praeger.
1969
—————. *A Short History of Socialism*. NY: Praeger Publishers.
1970
Likert, Rensis. *The Human Organization*. NY: McGraw-Hill.
1967
—————. *New Patterns of Management*. NY: McGraw-Hill.
1961
Lipset, Seymour M. *Political Man*. Garden City, N.Y.: Doubleday.
1960
Livingston, John C., and Robert G. Thompson. *The Consent of the Governed*.
1963   NY: Macmillan.
Lynd, Staughton. "No Supervision without Representation," *Working Papers
1974   for a New Society*, 2 (Summer): 16–22.
Macciocchi, Maria. *Daily Life in Revolutionary China*. NY: Monthly Review Press.
1972
Maccoby, Michael. "Changing Work: The Boliva Project." *Working Papers for
1975   a New Society*, 3 (Summer): 43–55.
Mallet, S. *Bureaucracy and Technology in the Socialist Countries*. Nottingham,
1972   England: Spokesman.
Mao Tse-Tung. *Selected Works*. Peking: Foreign Language Press.
1963
March, James G., and Herbert Simon. *Organizations*. NY: Wiley.
1958
Maslow, Abraham. *Eupsychian Management*. Homewood, Ill: Irwin-Dorsey.
1964
—————. *Motivation and Personality*. NY: Harper & Row.
1954
McEwan, John D. "The Cybernetics of Self-Organizing Systems." In C. George
1971   Benello and Dimitrios Roussopoulos (eds.), *The Case for Participatory
         Democracy*. New York: Viking: 179–194.
McGregor, Douglas. "The Scanlon Plan Through a Psychologist's Eyes." In Lesieur,
1958   1958:89–99.
McKitterick, T. E., and R. D. Roberts. *Workers and Management: The German
1953   Co-determination Experiment*. London: Gollancz.
Michels, Robert. *Political Parties, A Sociological Study of the Oligarchical Ten-
1958   dencies of Modern Democracy (1915)*. Glencoe, Ill: The Free Press.
Miller, James G. "Living Systems: Basic Concepts," *Behavioral Science*, 10 (July):
1965   193–237.
Mulder, Mauk. "Power Equalization Through Participation?" *Administrative Science
1971   Quarterly* 16 (March):31–40.
—————. "The Learning of Participation." *International Sociological Conference
1973   on Participation and Self-Management*, 4. Zagreb: Institute for Social
         Research:219–228.
Myers, Charles A. "Problems under the Plan—Summary: Personnel Session,"
1958   in Lesieur, 1958.

Myrdal, Jan.   *China: The Revolution Continued.* NY: Pantheon Books.
1970

National Industrial Conference Board.   Research Report #21: *Works Councils*
1919   *in the United States,* Boston: N.I.C.B.

National Industrial Conference Board.   Research Report #50: *Experience with*
1922   *Works Councils in the United States.* NY: Century Co.

National Industrial Conference Board.   *Collective Bargaining Through Employee*
1933   *Representation.* NY: Century Co.

NDP Ottawa Report.   Occasional publication of the New Democratic Party, Ottawa,
1973–75   Ontario: Office of the Federal Leader.

Newsweek.   "Who Wants to Work?" March 26.
1973

Norcross, Derek.   "Worker Participation." *Los Angeles Times,* March 9.
1975

Nordhoff, Charles.   *Communistic Societies of the U.S.* (1875). NY: Dover.
1972

Norton, John.   "Comments Concerning Worker Self-Management." Cambridge,
1974   Mass.: Harvard School of Business. Mimeographed.

Obradović, Josip.   "Participation and Work Attitudes in Yugoslavia," *Industrial*
1970   *Relations.* (February) 9:161–169.

O'Toole, James (ed.).   *Work and the Quality of Life.* Cambridge: MIT Press.
1974

Papanek, Jan.   *Czechoslovakia.* Boston: Appleton.
1946

Pateman, Carole.   *Participation and Democratic Theory.* Cambridge: Cambridge
1970   University Press.

Perrow, Charles.   *Complex Organizations: A Critical Analysis.* Englewood Cliffs,
1971   N.J.: Prentice-Hall.

Poor's Register of Corporations. N.Y.: Standard & Poors.
1970

Potvin, Raymond H.   *An Analysis of Labor-Management Councils in Belgian*
1958   *Industry.* Washington, D.C.: Catholic University of American Press.

Puckett, Elbridge.   "Measuring-Performance Under the Scanlon Plan." In Frederick
1958   G. Lesieur, 1958:65–79.

Remington, Robin (ed.).   *Winter in Prague: Czechoslovak Communism in Crisis.*
1969   Cambridge: MIT Press.

Richman, Barry.   *Industrial Society in Communist China.* NY: Random House.
1967

Rozner, Menachem.   "Principal Types and Problems of Direct Democracy in the
1965   Kibbutz." Givat Haviva: Social Research Center on the Kibbutz at Givat
         Hoviva, p. 1.

Rus, Veljko.   "The Limits of Organized Participation," *International Sociological*
1972   *Conference on Participation and Self-Management,* 2 Zagreb: Institute
         for Social Research:165–188.

Schrade, Paul.   Former western regional president, United Auto Workers, Personal
1974   communication, November.

Schuchman, Abraham.   *Codetermination: Labor's Middle Way in Germany.* Washing-
1957   ton, D.C.: Public Affairs Press.

Schultz, George.   "Worker Participation on Production Problems," In Lesieur,
1958   1958:50–64.

Schumacher, E. F.   *Small Is Beautiful: Economics as if People Mattered.* NY: Harper
1973   and Row.

Seeger, Murray.   "Socialists in Sweden Plan Third Step." *Los Angeles Times,*
1975   Part IX, November 16:1.

Shearer, Derek.   "North Moves Left: Politics in British Columbia." *Working Papers*
1974   *for a New Society,* 2 (Spring): 49–56.

Šik, Ota.   *Plan and Market under Socialism.* White Plains, NY: International Arts &
1971   Sciences Press.

Skinner, B. F.   *Science and Human Behavior.* NY: Basic Books.
1953

Smith, Adam.   *An Inquiry into the Nature and Causes of the Wealth of Nations*
1952   (*1776*). Chicago: William Benton and Encyclopedia Brittanica.

Smith, Patricia C., Lorne M. Kendall, and Charles L. Hulin.   *The Measurement of*
1969   *Satisfaction in Work and Retirement.* Chicago: Rand McNally.

Sprague, Blanche H.   "Bat'a, Chief Figure in the World's Shoe Industry," *Facts and*
1932   *Figures in Economic History.* Cambridge: Harvard University Press:276–303.

Steers, Richard M., and Lyman W. Porter, *Motivation and Work Behavior.* NY:
1975   McGraw-Hill.

Stradel, Karel.   "Choosing the General Manager: Democratization of the SKODA-
1969   Plzen Metallurgical Works," *Czechoslovak Life* (September):30–33.

Sturmthal, Adolf.   *Workers Councils: A Study of Workplace Organization on Both*
1964   *Sides of the Iron Curtain.* Cambridge: Harvard University Press.

—————.   "Workers' Participation in Management: USA." *International Institute*
1969   *of Labour Studies Bulletin.* No. 5:149–186.

Szulc, Tad.   *Czechoslovakia after World War II.* New York: Viking Books.
1972

Tabb, J. Yanai, and Amira Goldfarb.   "Workers' Participation in Management:
1970   Israel." International Institute of Labour Studies Bulletin No. 7.

Tannenbaum, Arnold S. and Robert A. Cooke. "Control and Participation", *Journal*
1974   *of Contemporary Business,* 3:35–46 (Autumn).

Theobald, Robert.   *Alternative America II.* Chicago: Swallow Press.
1970

Therborn, Goren.   Faculty of Sociology, University of Lund, Sweden. Personal
1974   communication. September.

Topham, Tony, and Fred Singleton.   "Yugoslav Workers' Control: The Latest Phase,"
New Left Review, 18.

Vanek, Jaroslav.   "Basic Theory of Financing of Participatory Firms," Internal Working
1972a   Paper of Program on Participation and Labor-Managed Systems. Ithaca:
Cornell University.

—————.   "Some Fundamental Considerations of Financing and the Right of
1972b   Property under Labor Management," Internal Working Paper of Program on
Participation and Labor-Managed Systems. Ithaca: Cornell University.

—————.   *The General Theory of Labor-Managed Market Economies.* Ithaca:
1970   Cornell University Press.

—————.   *The Participatory Economy: An Evolutionary Hypothesis and A Strategy*
1971   *for Development.* Ithaca: Cornell University Press.

Vernon, Raymond.   *Sovereignty at Bay: The Multinational Spread of U.S. Enterprises.*
1971   NY: Basic Books.

Walker, Kenneth F., and L. Grefié de Bellecombe.   "Workers' Participation in
1974   Management: Problems, Practice, and Prospect," *International Institute*
for Labour Studies (Geneva) Bulletin No. 12: 3ff.

Walton, Richard E.   "Alienation and Innovation in the Workplace," in James
1974a   O'Toole (ed.) *Work and the Quality of Life.* Cambridge, Mass.: MIT Press.

—————.   "Innovative Restructuring of Work," in Jerome M. Rosow (ed.), *The*
1974b   *Worker and the Job: Coping with Change.* Englewood Cliffs, N.J.: 145–176.

Whyte, William F.   *Money and Motivation: An Analysis of Incentives in Industry.*
1955   NY: Harper & Row.

Wilson, Harold B.   *Democracy and the Workplace.* Montreal: Black Rose Books.
1974

Woodward, Joan.   *Industrial Organization: Theory and Practice.* Cambridge:
1965   Oxford University Press.

Zimbalist, Andrew.   "Worker Participation in the Management of Socialized Industry:
1974   An Empirical Study of the Chilean Experience under Allende." Ph.D.
Dissertation, Harvard University, Department of Economics.

Zwerdling, Daniel.   "Looking for Workers' Control," *Working Papers for a New*
1974   *Society,* 2:11–15. (Autumn).

Index